Also by Leandro Herrero

The Leader with Seven Faces
Viral Change
New Leaders Wanted: Now Hiring!

dISRUPTIVE
idEAS

Disruptive Ideas

10+10+10=1000:
the maths of Viral Change
that transform organisations

Leandro Herrero

First published in 2008 by:
meetingminds
PO Box 1192, HP9 1YQ, United Kingdom
www.meetingminds.com

ISBN Paperback edition:
10 - Digit: 1-905776-04-7
13 - Digit: 978-1-905776-04-7

A CIP catalogue record for this title is available from the British Library

TABLE OF CONTENTS

2

Disruptive Ideas

Disruptive [management] ideas are those that have the capacity to create significant impact on the organisation by challenging standard management practices. They share the following characteristics:

1. They are simple.
2. There is a total disproportion between their simplicity and their potential to impact on and transform the life of organisations.
3. They can be implemented now.
4. You can implement them at little or no cost.
5. They are most likely to be contrarian.
6. They are also most likely to be counterintuitive.
7. They pose a high risk of being trivialised or dismissed.
8. They can spread virally within the organisation very easily.

You only need a few disruptive ideas to create big transformation without the need for a Big Change Management Programme. The impact of a combination of a few is just like dynamite.

Disruptive ideas provide management alternatives that, if spread, can completely transform the way the organisation works without the need to execute a massive 'change management programme'. Each of them, in its own right, has the potential to create significant change. The compound benefit of a few of them is a real engine of change and business transformation.

The concept of disruption in management has been applied to innovation before. A disruptive innovation is a technology, process or business model that introduces a much more affordable product or service (that is also much simpler to use) into a market.

It enables more consumers in that market to afford and/or have the skill to use the product or service. The change caused by such an innovation is so big that it eventually replaces, or disrupts, the established approach to providing that product or service. Disruptive Innovation as a concept was created by Clayton Christensen, author of *The Innovator's Dilemma* and *The Innovator's Solution*.

Leandro Herrero's disruptive ideas transcend innovation or technology and go back to the fundamental roots of day-to-day management in any kind of organisation, challenging conventional wisdom. In this book, Leandro Herrero's disruptive ideas are classified as structural, behavioural and process related.

Prologue:

The power of a few disruptive rules

Prologue:
The power of a few
disruptive rules

I have antibodies against the Big Corporate Initiative (or the Big Initiative in Big Corporations or, worse, the Big Initiative in not-so-Big Corporations that think they are Big or want to behave as Very Big). All over the world you can see the same picture: big change projects with lots of components, stacks of PowerPoint slides and massive communication programmes. In *Viral Change*, I called it the 'tsunami approach'.

As I will explain in the Introduction (which doubles as a summary of the Viral Change™ methodology and its conceptual background), a small set of behaviours has the power to create a culture or to change it.

Disruptive Ideas explains the maths of Viral Change™: the compound power of a small set of rules bringing true business transformation. Although this book complements *Viral Change™, the alternative to slow, painful and unsuccessful management of change in organisations*, it is self-contained and can be read independently.

In my consulting work on behavioural and cultural change, I often use a mental device that I call 'Imagine'. Imagine that this or that happens across the board in your organisation, that it is widespread. What kind of culture would you have? Can you picture it? And I follow up with a series of scenarios, each containing one behavioural pattern. For example, imagine your boss checking up on you every single day to see how you were doing in terms of meeting milestones in your project. Imagine people using little email and a lot of face-to-face or telephone. Imagine absolutely everybody using a Blackberry and responding immediately to every single email received. Imagine people making decisions in real time, without the need for a meeting with many other people (who were perhaps redundant to the decision anyway), etc.

Most of the scenarios either elicit a smile or raise eyebrows. It takes a millisecond for people to imagine hell or heaven and it only takes one single behaviour to do it. In my presentation to clients, I do not project a complex pattern of those behaviours on screen. I am also not asking them to react to a high level concept like 'an entrepreneurial culture' or 'a culture of mistrust'. I am simply talking behaviours, one by one. Each of them, on their own merits, may make people stay or leave the company; join it or avoid it. And I will repeat the key point: you only need one.

If one on its own is so powerful, why does the Big Corporate Programme insist we create, develop and 'roll out' dozens, if not hundreds of initiatives, divided into actions, critical success factors and personal goals?

10+10+10=1000

Even if you don't want to settle for just one of those behaviours or 'rules', the compound power of a small set of behaviours has tremendous impact. In this book, I offer you 10 ideas for 'structures', 10 for 'processes' and 10 for 'behaviours' from which you can choose. Even if you think that all of them are 'good ideas', you only need to choose a few. I am convinced that the sum of a few 'radical changes' with a small r can create Radical change with a big R. What do these 10s have in common?

- All of them are simple: you don't need a legion of consultants to implement them. Their simplicity directly correlates with their potential to transform the organisation.
- All of them can be triggered or acted upon tomorrow. They do not need to wait for the next cycle of the Strategic Plan or for when you have a budget.
- They can be implemented very cheaply, sometimes at zero cost. So when you consider their

potential to change the system (i.e., big time and for good), focusing energy on them is highly cost-effective!

■ Many of these ideas are contrarian because they represent an alternative way that opposes 'the normal way'. I believe we often practice 'management by default' and that we continue doing things as before, as we have always done, assuming rationality and logic in what we do. But sometimes it would be healthier to say, *"Errr, mmm, excuse me sir, no offence, but this emperor has no clothes. Perhaps the Contrarian Emperor has."*

■ Most of them are also counterintuitive. We are not used to doing things in different ways so the first impression of these ideas may be one of 'has no logic' or 'won't work'. And following that first impression is a great strategy to be 'safe'!

■ In isolation, many of them may look trivial, perhaps nothing more than a list of self-help ideas for the organisation! Or a prescriptive list: do this and you'll be OK. If you read them and think 'what's the big deal?', you either live in organisational nirvana, or you are content with what you have (nothing wrong with that), or you are still stuck in Big Corporate mode, looking down from the summit from where all things look small. You may also think that they are plain common sense, and as such, follow the rule that common sense is the least common of all the senses. We tend to say 'sure, of course' to many 'common sense things' and then switch off and carry on regardless.

■ All of them have high viral change potential. That is, you don't have to communicate to everybody on earth that you are implementing them. All you need to do is start somewhere and have people adopt the idea(s) so that others will follow.

Many of these disruptive ideas may perhaps seem obvious (in what they can do, should do, the problem they attempt to tackle). For those of you feeling this way, may I remind you of the Latin etymology of the word obvious: in the way. It means something so common right in front of you that you don't even see it and you stumble, trip and fall. Beware of the obvious things on the road, they can make life dangerous. All of them come from my personal experience as an organisational architect. So all are tested, all work ... and you may already know this, because perhaps you are already doing some of them!

There are many people in the organisational and business worlds looking for The Big Idea. I prefer to collect small ideas with big impact. The type of management of change that I facilitate and practice, Viral Change™, shows that a small set of behaviours, spread by a small number of people through the informal networks of the organisation, creates behavioural tipping points through which a new way of doing things appears and is established. The introduction on the next pages explains why and how. Although the 10+10+10 are three sets of 'structures', 'processes' and 'behaviours', let's make one thing clear: you must look at behaviours as your real currency to create change and transform the organisation. Structures and processes per se won't do it.

Book structure

- This book is a long conversation with you, citizen of any business organisation, manager, leader, manager-postulant, manager-novice, Head of HR, non-head of HR...basically with anybody who wants to energise the company and inject some new maths of change.
- Other than this prologue and introduction, the 10+10+10=1000 'rules' are written as a series of thirty short, self-contained chats...as if they came up as part of a brainstorm between us. They do not intend to explore the rule or idea in depth, but to leave behind enough of a disruptive or contrarian challenge for you to carry on the thought process and imagine the application of the idea to your organisation. I would encourage you to use the blank spaces in this book as much as possible to make notes or plan. This is your live book of planning for the transformation of your organisation.
- Each 'short chat'/chapter has a few paragraphs entitled 'Imagine'. This is for you to imagine and literally picture the culture of the organisation once some of those 'rules' were in place. The

paragraphs written in each chapter are illustrative. You should continue the thought process and add your own notes.

- I do not believe that you need to be in a big organisation for these ideas to be implemented. Even small and medium enterprises can benefit from these ideas.

- I have compiled a map of the 3 sets of 10 (10+10+10) at the end of the book so that you can play personal monopoly and decide on which ones you want to put your money!

Disruptive ideas are like a butterfly's wings: they seem trivial, but have the potential to create a hurricane. Please read and enjoy these butterflies. The chapters are self-contained and can therefore be read independently and in any order, but I suggest you read the Introduction first.

Good luck with the transformation, but above all, watch out for 'the obvious things on your way'... those things can be treacherous.

Introduction:

Changing the way we think about change

Introduction: Changing the way we think about change

A small set of rules, particularly a small set of behaviours, has the power to create significant and sustainable change in the organisation.

This statement - crucial to understanding the type of change management that I have labelled Viral Change™ - is based upon three premises:

1. Life in the organisation is not linear. What do I mean by this? Every day in the organisation, we see things that show a disproportion between what we consider cause and effect. Take trust, for example. It usually takes a lot to build. It looks like a slow growth curve. Suddenly, something happens (an event, a reward, acknowledgement of error and show of honesty at the top...) and trust levels rocket. It may stay like this for a long time. Then, something else happens - perhaps only a relatively

small breach, in the broad context - and trust is quickly eroded, slipping down the curve and often leaving behind a strong sense of injustice and feeling of unfairness.

The reality is that sometimes, whether we like it or not, small interventions ('disruptions') have a big impact or huge repercussions. This non-linear context, in which we work every day, is vital to understanding change in organisations. However, most of the 'change management' frameworks we are familiar with – and most planning and implementation processes, for that matter - assume the opposite, i.e. linearity: big problems need big solutions, big changes need big interventions, big goals need a big number of strategic objectives and a big number of actions and implementations.

2. Let's dig a bit deeper into change. Many experienced managers would agree that there is no real change unless we see a change in behaviours. We can design new structures, create massive communication plans, map new processes and systems, train people and then call it change. But if people continue working like before or if their behaviours have not changed much, then all we have is the illusion of change. The problem is that the main assumption - tacit or explicit - behind 'processes and change' is a

flawed one: that is, behaviours will follow as a consequence of change in processes. We had A, we changed to B because it is better; people will behave accordingly. As many people know, that doesn't happen ... at least, not all the time!

The above assumption is wrong. Behaviours are misplaced in the equation. New processes and systems do not create behaviours in a sustainable way. Even an initial peak of positive reaction is often followed by fading interest and low adoption. The fact is that simply reactive change in behaviours following the implementation of a new process or system is often unsustainable. On the contrary, we need to have those behaviours in the organisation first in order to sustain a new process!

Let's look at an example. Imagine that you are introducing 'collaborative software', a system that enables people to share information, create common repositories, share ideas and plans, continuously update customer data, etc. The new system may not create collaboration per se. It will not convert individualistic people into gregarious collaborators. It will not make people input data into the CRM (customer relationship management) system just because they can. Collaborative behaviour somehow needs to be pre-existing in the behavioural fabric of the organisation. Then the 'collaborative software' will facilitate collaboration in a sustainable way. The software needs the process first, the process needs the behaviours first ... so, behaviours must come first.

These days, new Web 2.0 technology, such as social networks, blogs or wikis, has more capacity than any other previous technology to trigger new behaviours. Facebook, YouTube, SMS... they all *generate* behaviours, so the above relationship between process, technology and behaviours has become a bit more complex. For the first time we have technologies that are 'simple' and 'pervasive' and, above all, training-less. If people within the firm have the ability to communicate on an internal blog and they can grasp the benefits almost on the spot, then a minimal critical mass of adopters may suddenly appear to be creating a true 'behavioural tipping point' where blog-communication has become the norm. In that sense, technology (the blog) created the behaviours (fast communication and fast participation) and a new process for collaboration (real time fluid discussion without email) was born. However, two things need to be taken into consideration here:

(a) Some sort of collaborative behaviour was already present in terms of needs. The existence of the blog per se was not going to change the behaviours of people who weren't interested in sharing any idea.

(b) Even if collaboration was triggered (because people 'needed' it and jumped at the opportunity), sustaining it would soon be dependent not on the continuous availability of the technology (it will still be there), but on the reinforcement of the behaviours, that is, the benefits associated with the behaviours of people communicating in that way.

3. To paraphrase Margaret Thatcher (*"there is no such thing as society"*), I would say that there is no such thing as culture, there are only behaviours. Behaviours create culture, not the other way around. Culture is not a closed container of things such as beliefs, attitudes, values, behaviours and logos. Intellectually it may be stimulating to use all these terms - they make for good conversations - but pragmatically, other than the visible logo (as a shortcut to 'a culture'), the only observable things are behaviours. A culture of accountability, for example, does not exist in the same way as an HR department or a Performance Management system. Seeing people doing A,B,C (taking responsibility for actions, keeping promises, reacting to problems quickly and being rewarded for clear outcomes) - thereby behaving in a

specific manner - allows us to label that culture in such a way.

The same applies to any other 'culture'. 'Culture of innovation' is a good, appealing and engaging concept, but beyond the language itself, it's not a terribly effective, operational one. What we see is people doing innovative things, improving the way they solve problems, coming up with new ideas, routinely asking themselves, "*can we do this differently?*", etc. It is precisely because of the collective existence of these behaviours in a particular organisation that we can allow ourselves to label it a 'culture of innovation', not because there is an 'innovation container' where these things reside. You may argue that if these behaviours do exist, it's surely because the place must have processes, systems, rules, etc. that allow or facilitate people to behave in those ways. This is true, but those processes, systems and rules have been created by individuals; they are the output of their behaviours. Some people create the rules for other people to be able to do innovative things; other people follow them. In both cases, we are talking behaviours.

These three premises - (1) the non-linearity of the organisation, (2) the need to focus on behaviours to create and declare 'real change' and (3) the understanding of culture as a concept which only makes sense through visible behaviours - allow us to establish the fundamental basis for an alternative, modern approach to management of change. This is Viral Change™, which I have introduced before with the statement that 'under certain conditions, a small set of behaviours has the power to create significant change'.

The next question must be the 'how'. To answer this, we have to start by questioning how we could define that small set of behaviours. Let me say upfront that any behaviour needs reinforcement (reward, recognition) in order to become stable. Put differently: if behaviour A is there, it is because it's being reinforced (whether we know what or who is reinforcing it or not). So if we need to reinforce the behaviours belonging to that small set, we need to define them at a level that can be easily reinforced. What level is this? It is rather detailed and concrete with unequivocal meaning for all people involved. Let's look at an example. Collaboration is certainly a behaviour, but left at that conceptual level, two people may easily have different interpretations of what it means. And even worse, they may not double-check their understanding of the meaning and tacitly assume that they are both talking about the same thing. This high level concept - which I have called macromolecular to use a biological analogy - is not very helpful in terms of reinforcement. These two people may be rewarding different or even opposing things under the same collaboration banner.

If we try to be more specific, people may come up with some further translations. For example, for X, collaboration is the sharing of information between teams and for Y it's the spontaneous sharing of resources when needed. This level is now beginning to look more susceptible to reinforcement, because I am bound to see whether the information and/or the resources are shared and which people do so. I have called this level 'molecular'. The same people discussing this - now perhaps having gained a better understanding of this challenge - may want to go even further and say, for example, that the real behaviours they would like to see are people from team A sending a weekly email to all members of team B with updated information on customers and that the leaders of A and B meet every Monday to 'lend resources' to each other. I call this level of behaviours 'atomic'.

This atomic level, viewed out of context may appear trivial, particularly to anybody who is not part of the exercise... But within the greater context - that is, having atomic behaviours that create molecular ones and molecular behaviours that create high level macromolecular concepts - these atomic behaviours are far from trivial. The test of the validity of atomic behaviours is simple. It only requires management judgement and imagination. The question to be asked is: "*Imagine that everybody does* (insert atomic behaviour here), *that it becomes the norm, a routine. What kind of organisation would we be building?*" This 'imagine' test is at the core of the way we need to map this small set of behaviours.

Depending on the circumstances of the organisation or the goals of the 'change management programme', you - perhaps with some guidance from people with a strong behavioural sciences background - will come up with a list of potential behaviours, all of them passing your 'imagine' test.

The next step is choice. My words are used carefully. I don't say prioritisation, although this is certainly one way of choosing. The difference, however, is relevant. In our traditional prioritisation process, we perhaps define what is achievable or not, or what can be done with the resources available. Narrowing down the choices often entails abandoning all those good ideas that are 'not under our control' or would be too costly. Unfortunately, this approach means that in many cases, the ones that could make the biggest impact slip through the net. These considerations may be important but in my experience, people dismiss ideas on this basis too often and too quickly. With the behavioural focus - as opposed to the process focus - there is much we can do even without direct control of some resources.

In Viral Change™ mode, we invite management to exercise judgement and choose behaviours mainly driven by the 'imagine' test. In my consulting experience with organisations, a small set of four to six behaviours defined at atomic level and passing the 'imagine' test is all we need to create big change.

Still in the 'how', we need to add another principle: that is, the organisation is a network of connections (flow of information + influence). This is hardly a groundbreaking statement. However, most management practices and 'change management process' do nothing more than pay lip service to it, whilst focusing energy and attention on a concept of the organisation that resembles a 'plumbing system' with leadership at the top and goals, guidelines, rules and data percolating down the pipes through all management levels. This rather mechano-hydraulic – input at the top, output at the bottom - concept of the organisation includes the existence of groupings of people with common goals, called teams. In fact, the default concept of the organisation is one of being a teamocracy. We have been taught that teams are the natural form of collaboration and management practices have internalised this fully to the extent that we happily and more or less unconsciously equate collaboration and team.

However, the modern view of the organisation is more one of an often loose network of connections between individuals. Yes, some of those connections have been designed and manufactured in order to achieve performance (teams, committees, task forces), but these may only account for a quarter of the total. It is like visiting a new city and jumping on a bus tour. You see the monuments, the buildings of the institutions, the main streets and parks and some curiosities. This hardly gives you

Introduction

a profound understanding of city life. In reality, many citizens may spend their entire productive city life without stepping into any of those buildings, streets or parks. The bus tour of the organisation shows us teams and structures, but there is a lot more going on. Informal conversations, spontaneous collaboration, tapping into intellectual capital outside the borders of 'my team', asking questions, starting a conversation on a common worrying issue, venting emotions (including whinging, frustration, incredulity or admiration), etc. occur in the networks of individuals, the real highways of the organisation.

Some of those connections are 'strong ties' (close, frequent) and others are 'weak ties' (distant, loose, occasional) as defined by sociologists. Most - but not all - of the strong type groupings are represented by the teams. These are the designed and visible spaces of collaboration. But perhaps up to three quarters of the organisational life is only understood in the context of those highways of looser and perhaps invisible connections where 'conversations happen'.

Today, we know quite a lot about how networks work, thanks to a captivating convergence of social sciences and computer sciences. There are remarkable similarities between those networks, whether they are ones providing the connections on the worldwide web, computer networks or social networks such as the ones that truly represent the organisational life. I believe that three characteristics of those networks have fascinating consequences for the management of the organisation and the management of change.

First of all, the network is not terribly democratic and equalitarian. A few nodes (individuals) have loads of connections and most of the other nodes (individuals) have fewer connections. It is far from the usual Bell curve or normal distribution that constantly comes to mind when we ask ourselves any question about performance of people in the organisation. In fact, it is better represented by a power law or logarithmic distribution. Incidentally, this characteristic – well-demonstrated both in the e-world and the social world - should hardly be a surprise for people working in organisations. The fact that a relatively small number of individuals, not necessarily high in the hierarchical ranks, seem to be very well connected is a 'street observation'.

The second characteristic is even less egalitarian. Those nodes (individuals) with a high number of connections tend to acquire even more; and those with fewer connections tend to stay like this or even have progressively less (unless some sort of 'personal mutation' happens). Again, this is unsurprising; another formulation for 'the rich get richer (in connections, power, influence) and the poor get poorer'. I have called this the Matthew effect of networks ("*For unto every one that hath shall be given, and he shall have abundance: but from him that hath not shall be taken away even that which he hath*" – Matthew XXV:29, KJV).

The third characteristic is that at some point in the life of those nodes, some of them will stop behaving as individual nodes and will adopt a collective single unitary behaviour. A tipping point occurs and a new entity or phenomenon appears. This is a complicated way of explaining how water molecules turn to ice at zero degrees - phase transition in physics. Extrapolating with some liberty to social life, the individuals of a team may stop being individuals with differentiated thinking, only to see one, single, unified, strong and internally cohesive reality. We call it 'groupthink'.

If we put these three characteristics together – power law, Matthew effect and tipping points - and then apply them to the organisational life, a fantastic and enlightening picture appears. Effectively, a small group of individuals holds the power to influence the rest of the organisation, but they can hardly be represented by the hierarchy shown on the organisation chart. This group or sector of the network will grow in their influence over time (although their membership may change). If these highly connected, highly influential people took on board the spread of that small set of behaviours that passed the 'imagine' test, endorsed them, practiced them, encouraged others to do the same and reinforced those behaviours when they saw them (peer to peer), then, at some stage of that progression of influence, a 'social-phase-transition' (tipping point) would occur and those behaviours would become established as a new routine.

We may not see the transition, in the same way that we do not see the water molecules turning into ice! People who have been influenced can now influence others - with a power consistent with their degree of connectivity - and again at some point, some clusters of individuals will have enough critical mass to 'tip' and establish a new routine or behavioural norm. Change under these circumstances takes the form of an internal epidemic of new behaviours, a true social infection, not a cascaded down 'training' or communication programme with a series of presentations and workshops.

So, who are those 'powerful people'? How can we find them and ask them for help? There are many ways - with different degrees of sophistication – at our disposal to identify those people. The academic, social sciences way is to use tools to perform what is called a 'social network analysis' or mapping of those connections, which can be done via questionnaires or other means. My 'practitioner's way' is to simply ask people! In my consulting experience, if you ask senior management for a particular profile of individuals – highly connected, great influence, people listen to them, what they do matters and is sometimes imitated, may be in lower ranks, etc. – they are able to write down names almost on the spot. It is a less sophisticated, more pragmatic way to 'find' those people, who will be asked to help in the spreading of new behaviours.

The mechanisms for that spread are well-known in social sciences: imitation, social copying, role modelling, etc. In practical terms, it means Joe having a conversation with Lisa in terms like this: "*You know, I think it is about time we take this seriously and keep our promises. I am certainly going to start. At the next meeting, I am going to propose that we check with each other for any broken promises. What do you think? I am all for it.*" This may be a small and simplistic example, but in Viral Change™ mode all starts with initial endorsement and role modelling from that small set of highly connected individuals, which I tend to label 'Change Champions' or 'Change Agents'.

Whilst at individual and micro-social level, the main vehicle of propagation is imitation, social copying or conformity with 'a new rule' established by somebody (or a group) one trusts, at macro-social level (still within the organisation) the main vehicle is the story. What has worked or not, how a team overcame a bureaucratic barrier, how another grouped bypassed the 'lack of data' in order to act, what John did in Scotland with a sceptical customer, how meetings have completely changed in that Unit by adapting the agenda to the new required behaviours, how people in that group in Cornwall systematically pick up the phone and ask peers in East Anglia for input or ideas, etc. ... these are the kind of things people remember and tend to imitate or 'bookmark'. It may sound as the practice of 'Best Practices', but it isn't. 'Best Practices' are often project focused and rather static, only reviewed annually or at planned times. Stories flow every day and can be spread at any time producing a constant stream of 'things that are now happening and that weren't there before'.

We can now see how Viral Change™ is very different from the standard 'me-too change management programme'. In the standard, conventional way, a big set of actions, communicated to all, more or less at the same time, at all management levels, is expected to reach every corner of the organisation and produce change. In Viral Change™ mode, a small set of behaviours, spread via internal networks of influence, by a small group of people, create an internal infection and behavioural tipping points leading to sustainable changes, further spread by stories.

Three further characteristics of Viral Change™ also need to be taken into account:

(a) The measure of success is not done via the usual set of milestones and deadlines. In fact, a metrics system needs to be created from scratch and tailored to the organisation, including those elements of the 'imagine' test that the organisation wants to 'see'. With the traditional 'me-too' programme, everything is mapped up front, timetabled and 'predicted'. With the Viral Change™ approach, it is appropriate to construct fit-for-purpose metrics once the process has started and the champions themselves can play a big role in that mapping. The metrics system may contain some quantitative data, but it is likely to be constructed mainly on a qualitative basis, based upon the flow of stories. This is not the usual way that heavily process-driven organisations 'measure things' and it may need some effort to understand and adjust management's mindset. As Einstein said, *"Not everything that can be counted counts and not everything that counts can be counted."*

(b) Viral Change™ challenges leadership models in the organisation, since what's required here is backstage support to the champions' community in their spread of the infection. In fact, a model of 'distributed leadership' emerges and suddenly the organisation becomes 'leader rich' with its champion's community. Top-down leadership must facilitate, support and enable the hidden work of the champions. There is no command and control involved with this community. In fact, if you push me in terms of defining a hierarchical line, the champions community reports directly to - and have a mandate from - the top leadership team, regardless of where the individual champion sits in a particular line management structure within the 'plumbing system'.

(c) The word 'hidden' in the paragraph above is not trivial. Viral Change™ occurs in a rather informal and invisible way, like an infection. There are no workshops where line managers brief the champions or a myriad of PowerPoints cascaded down. Champions may want to meet with people, but that will be on their own initiative and it will be informal. (Again, leadership needs to facilitate this by removing barriers or enabling some resources). There are no big declarations of 'a new programme' or anything that looks/may look like 'another corporate initiative'. The more visible and more formal Viral Change™ becomes, the less likely its success. Invisibility doesn't mean secrecy. The aims can be well stated by the top leadership as a one-off, but afterwards the less we talk and the more we act the better. Also, informality doesn't mean chaos. It means allowing informal conversations and facilitating the non-formal, non-structured life of the organisation. In fact, the greatest risk to Viral Change™ is the almost inevitable tendency to formalise it more than needed; something that sometimes occurs spontaneously in the management ranks due to our learned way of doing things.

This is not to say that with Viral Change™ there is no structure or organisation involved. In fact, most of the things described here require some planning and a small team backstaging, coordinating and facilitating the optimum environment. For example, champions need to be identified and called in to help; they need to be gathered and presented with the ideas, the new behaviours and the way we propose them to work. Periodical gatherings of this community are needed to extract stories and track progress. Line management needs to be briefed on what is expected from them and, more importantly, what is not expected – such as directly managing the champions in their divisions, etc. So there is still a fair amount of social engineering required, but not on the scale of the traditional cascade down 'the plumbing system'.

In summary, Viral Change™ provides a different framework for the creation and spread of change which is sustained by both theory and practice. On the theoretical side, it has solid foundations in social sciences, behavioural sciences and modern network theory (the latter itself being built from computer sciences and complexity theory). On the practical side, we have significant experiences of this approach working in practical terms. For example, a collaborative environment, created in three to six months, still established and sustainable after three years.

Let me finally update the original premises at the beginning of this introduction and summarise the key ingredients of Viral Change™, both premises and distinctive actions:

1. The organisation is not linear, so it makes sense to look for small interventions ('disruptions') with potentially big impact. This book provides you with 30 different 'disruptions' to choose from! 10 of them have been categorised as structural, 10 as process based and 10 as behavioural. You don't need all 30. In fact, you must choose the ones that, when combined, can create the organisational change you're aiming for. The way to make those choices is simple: imagine! Imagine your

organisation once the chosen disruptive structure or process or behaviour or combinations thereof have been implemented! As mentioned in the prologue, each chapter has a few paragraphs inviting you to imagine and literally picture if this is where you want to go. Those paragraphs are there as an illustration and invitation to you to embellish the picture with your own imagination.

2. Behaviours are the only real currency for change. The book provides you with 10 of them as a suggestion, taken from my experience because of their capacity to introduce change in a significant way. But remember that the 10 (disruptive) structures and the 10 (disruptive) processes are de facto hiding other behaviours. When you choose Structures or Processes you must do so by imagining what the organisation (culture) would look like after those structures and processes have been implemented, in terms of how people would behave differently. In other words, Structures and Processes are here to create change and - if there is no change unless there is a change in behaviours - then those structures and processes must have the capacity to trigger, induce or facilitate behaviours, because behaviours are the only thing you will be able to see/reinforce. As we said before on the example of collaboration, if people have no interest whatsoever in collaborating, you'll need to engineer a way of inducing 'a taste of it', so that the behaviour is visible enough to be reinforceable.

3. A small, reinforceable set of those behaviours needs to be chosen. In the end, you may perhaps need five or six or eight... Some of them may come from the list of 10 behaviours and others may have been 'discovered' as underlying to some of the 10 structures or 10 processes. The short 'Imagine' section in each of those chapters will point you in the direction of some behaviours. So, for your organisation, you may for example be choosing 2 ideas/rules from 'structures', 3 from 'processes' and 2 from 'behaviours'. Now you have your dynamite! You will implement the new 'structures' and 'processes' in a way that will seed, trigger or 'create' some behaviours. I have said before that processes do not create sustainable behaviours per se, but they may trigger them and then they will need to be reinforced. So simply implementing the 2 new structures and the 3 processes without looking at the behaviours behind them will render your dynamite inexplosive in no time.

4. The spread of those behaviours occurs via internal networks of connections - mostly rather invisible – and, more effectively, through the initial influence of a small set of individuals (champions). These are the dimensions that I referred to at the beginning when I used the term 'under certain circumstances'. I strongly recommend you to consider the champions model if your chosen combination of structures + processes + behaviours requires changes that need to be spread

across the organisation. (See my book, *Viral Change*, for a description of how the champions' model works.)

5. New behaviours travel via stories and change takes place as an internal epidemic of success. Spend time describing how the combination of whatever number of structures, processes and behaviours you chose, made any difference and spread those stories as much as you can.

6. Measuring success is an ongoing effort through qualitative data and tailored metrics

7. If you choose the champions model of Viral Change™, leadership is distributed across the organisation, with formal leaders and managers playing a role of support and facilitation, not one of command and control.

8. Viral Change™ as a process must be fairly invisible and informal for it to work. However, that invisibility and informality needs to be crafted. These characteristics are counterintuitive to the traditional organisation and management may need to adjust their mindset. I strongly suggest that once you have chosen the combination of structures, processes and behaviours, you do not create a massive communication programme about them but make them spread via imitation. This is where a champions' community, even if small, can help a lot.

9. The main risk of failure comes from too much structure and the natural tendency to revert to a standard 'change management programme', in which we talk a lot about the programme and spend less time making sure that changes are happening. To achieve success, you must choose your combination of ideas from within the 10+10+10 and 'just do it'!

10. See the opportunity of creating specific cultural changes through the 10+10+10=1000 rule as an opportunity to question your concept of the organisation itself, your leadership practices and the capacity of your leaders to navigate through levels of ambiguity that are necessary for a more agile enterprise. An organisation with less command and control and where life is a constantly emerging discovery of possibilities beyond what is formally written, planned, measured, communicated and celebrated.

Structures

Structures 1

Team 365:
the team that
(almost) doesn't meet

One of the most toxic practices in organisational life is equating 'team' and 'team meeting'. You could start a true transformation by simply splitting them as far apart as you can and by switching on the team permanently. In a perfect team, 'stuff happens' all the time without the need to meet. Try the disruptive idea 'Team 365' to start a small revolution.

In our minds, the idea that teams are something to do with meetings is well embedded. And indeed, teams do meet... But 'the meeting' has become synonymous with 'the team'. Think of the language we often use. If there is an issue or something that requires a decision and this is discussed amongst people who belong to a team, we often hear things such as, "*let's bring it to the team*". In fact, what people mean really is, "*let's bring it to the meeting. Put it on the agenda.*" By default, we have progressively concentrated most of the 'team time' in 'meeting time'. The conceptual borders of these two very different things have become blurred. We have created a culture where team equals meetings equals team. And this is disastrous.

If you plan activities for a team, chances are that you are de facto planning *meetings* and putting them on calendars: every month, every quarter, onsite, offsite... Inevitably, team life is progressively taken over by meeting time and its associated paraphernalia: prepare agenda, ask for items, decide venue, send invitations, have the meeting, take minutes, distribute the minutes... If you were to chart team life, it would look like a series of peaks (meetings), separated by times of silence and times of build-up.

'Stuff happens' at meetings, or so we think. So, you'd better be there! This concentration of energy, anxiety, performance, mind power, theatre, emotions and all other ingredients for the meeting-cookout also has an unintended side-effect. If the meeting is where 'stuff happens', I need to make sure that somebody representing my department (or my division or me) will be there. 'Representational teams' are the norm in many organisations. I call them 'Ambassadorial teams', consisting of people not representing themselves, but the group/division.

Some of them even have something to say. Others are there 'just in case'. Have a look at your organisation and see if you may have created a culture of over-inclusiveness. A culture where teams are not only at the core of collaboration (literally hijacking other forms), but also one where there are crowds of 'ambassadors' moving around, meeting regularly and returning to their quarters with different degrees of commitment and different-sized lists of actions. You may actually have quite a lot of intellectual tourism.

As a consequence of the mental model and practice that reads 'teams = meeting = teams', the team member merely becomes an event traveller (from a few doors down or another country?). These team travellers bring packaged information, all prepared for the disclosure or discussion at 'the event'. Once the package is delivered, the information downloaded and the decision made (if lucky), the concept of team membership and its intensity fade. The sense of belonging has been hijacked by the meeting itself. And so, after the meeting, there is a void, waiting to be filled by the next call for items for the next agenda.

Imagine now the opposite scenario, where the concept of membership is one of 24 hours a day, 7 days a week, 365 days a year. And that this is when 'the real stuff happens', not at the meetings!

In 'team 365' mode, the meeting is an occasional event, something that happens when needed. It's not the centre of activity for the team. Instead, the emphasis is on the team as a continuous collaboration structure. The meeting is merely a device for occasional needs. Literally, Team 365 is always meeting, so it doesn't really need to meet. Well, almost.

Many people will see the above as a caricature. Sensible people will agree that the meeting is not the centre of the universe and that team life is a continuous endeavour. But this is very often just a politically correct answer. In many cases, the reality - and I suggest you look at your organisation with your eyes and mind wide open - is that team meetings have a huge magnetic effect and de facto suck the life out of organisational life. We have simply got the balance wrong. The meeting is a means, not an end in itself. Many organisations behave as if the opposite were true. How can you change things?

- Make your teams operate in 365-day, 'continuous meeting' mode and declare the formal team meeting a secondary activity that takes place only when needed. Invert the equation: the meeting should be the anomaly.
- 75% or more of the decisions that a team needs to make, don't need a formal meeting of all the team's members. Establish the rule that people who are empowered to make a decision, should make it in real time without needing to wait for a formal slot on the agenda of the next 'team meeting'.

- Most of the routine sharing of information and ongoing tracking of progress in any project can be done online by using a simple (or complex) electronic tool. Shared drives on your server are an obvious (old-fashioned) way of having a single repository of information. Your firm may be a bit more sophisticated these days and have some sort of document management system or 'e-room' where teams can store documentation including minutes. Today, enterprise wikis allow for on the spot continuous editing. The days of emails going back and forth with different versions of documents (such as agendas or minutes) circulating for approval are gone.

- In team 365, the project leader is also a 'project leader 365', not just the information traffic warden pre, during and post-meeting. Project leaders facilitate continuous discussion and the working together of members, whether in duos, trios or bigger groups. If people need to collaborate, they'll do it any time, not just at the meeting. If decisions need to be made, they can be made at any time, not just at the meeting. All will be transparent and posted in a common repository. The project leader takes care of the continuous flow of information.

- People sometimes use a catchphrase in meetings to express that something doesn't belong in the meeting; that it deserves to be dealt with outside the meeting, perhaps because it is complex. In jargon, that translates into: "*we will discuss this off-line*". Now think of the team as permanently 'off-line'. And the more things can be dealt with 'off-line', the less need there is for the meeting. So, ask yourself and your colleagues the magic question: "*do we really need a meeting for this?*" You will be amazed how many times the answer is, "*not really...*"

■ Can you still have any team meetings at all? Yes, but not as we know them. Meet with colleagues to explore and increase the social understanding of the behavioural fabric of the team. Talk processes and behaviours. Talk strategy. Celebrate successes. Debate when an issue requires a face-to-face (or virtual face-to-face). The meeting now primarily has a social goal. Period.

■ Team membership is team membership. There is no such thing as 'core members' and 'extended members'. If you need to call upon people's expertise from time to time, that doesn't make them 'extended team members'. They are people occasionally called upon. Most of the 'extended members' are often intellectual tourists or ambassadors. Many of them would be pleased to be de-listed as members and relieved from presenteism duties (and if they're not, you may wonder how busy or needed they really are in their day jobs).

AIM AT HAVING TEAMS THAT DO NOT (NEED TO) MEET, BECAUSE THEY ARE 'ALWAYS ON'.

IF YOU DO MEET WITH THE WHOLE TEAM, DO SO FOR 'SOCIAL REASONS', TO ENHANCE ALIGNMENT, TO DISCUSS STRATEGY AND NOT TO 'DO THE WORK'.

COLLABORATION, INFORMATION SHARING, PROJECT TRACKING AND DECISIONS: ALL TO HAPPEN IN REAL TIME, NOT AT MEETINGS.

GET RID OF TEAM= MEETING.

A TEAM MEMBER = A TEAM MEMBER. GET RID OF 'CORE' AND 'EXTENDED'.

THE BEST TEAM IS THE ONE THAT DOESN'T NEED TO MEET. AIM HIGH FOR THAT.

50

Your own ideas/plans

....

....

....

....

....

....

....

....

....

....

....

....

....

....

....

....

....

....

....

....

Imagine...

Imagine you have very few meetings. Imagine that teams in your organisation are involved in continuous activity, with people working together all the time under a leadership that puts people and ideas together. Imagine a culture where meetings are an anomaly and when they happen, they are enjoyable and useful as social glue and not a burden. Imagine a culture where decisions are made in real time without waiting for meetings; where transparent information on what is going on is always there with the same clarity and availability as logging in to the BBC news' homepage. Imagine that the excuse "*I haven't been informed*" no longer exists. Imagine that the expression 'bring it to the team' is an oxymoron: you are the team and can't bring it to yourself; you are in 'always on' mode. Imagine that you start somewhere in the organisation and spread the idea virally....

In your organisation

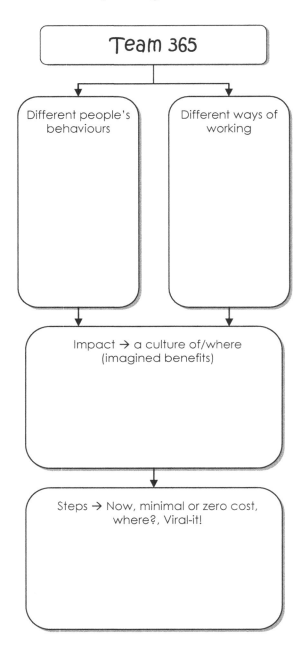

```
                    ┌──────────────────────┐
                    │       Team 365       │
                    └──────────────────────┘
         ┌────────────────────┐   ┌────────────────────┐
         │ Different people's  │   │ Different ways of  │
         │     behaviours      │   │     working        │
         │                     │   │                    │
         └────────────────────┘   └────────────────────┘
              ┌──────────────────────────────────┐
              │  Impact → a culture of/where      │
              │      (imagined benefits)          │
              │                                   │
              └──────────────────────────────────┘
              ┌──────────────────────────────────┐
              │  Steps → Now, minimal or zero cost,│
              │      where?, Viral-it!            │
              │                                   │
              └──────────────────────────────────┘
```

| Structures 2 |

Double hats (one boss is not enough)

There is nothing better than seeing the world through more than one pair of glasses. Usually organisations only give us one single pair. And definitely only one hat: your role, your function, your place in the organisation chart. And probably one silo. Dividing brain power over different responsibilities is incredibly effective and disruptively healthy in organisational life.

You are the manager of A or the director of B. Full stop. Here is the job description, here is the budget, here is the staff and off you go. This is your hat. We are supposed to wear our hat and our glasses all the time. The hat decides lots of things: which management team you belong to, which meetings you attend, which division you are part of and perhaps how much money you get every month. The better you wear that one hat, the more successful you are supposed to become. Small detail, this doesn't only apply to you, but also to another 200 or 3000 people. So the organisation definitely has plenty of single hats.

In your life outside of work, chances are you wear more than one hat. For example: father, sport coach, husband, secretary of club X or governor at a school board. Perhaps you're also a language student in the evenings. You are used to seeing things from different perspectives and to changing hats during the day, sometimes several times in one single afternoon! But when you go back to work the next day, you only have one hat from 9. 00 am onwards!

The business equivalent of you wearing several hats in your life outside of work would be to be simultaneously responsible for multiple functions or activities or projects. And my rule is, the more the different hats compete with each other, the better for you and for the organisation. Let's focus on senior management for a moment, because they are an easy example. Somebody may be in charge of country X as country manager. As such, in the context of his pan-European, multinational company, he is focused on the profit and loss (P&L) of country X. This is what he is paid for. This is his hat (and you may argue that wearing this hat is more than enough!). Now imagine that there is a pan-European marketing function that takes care of brands across Europe: all brands, all countries. What is good for country X may or may not be good for country Y, at least in the implementation of brand strategy. Each country manager is only concerned about his market. The centralised marketing structure is supposed to take care of all and accommodate for all.

There is nothing better in these dynamics than making country manager X responsible not only for the P&L of country X, but also, at the same time, for brand A in all European countries, whether directly or as sponsor of a centralised marketing team. You can already see the dynamics starting to work. Country manager X now de facto has 2 hats. With one, he must take care of what is good for his country. With the other hat, he must take into consideration what is good for all the countries. Both interests may or may not coincide.

Imagine that this pattern of competitive hats is a widespread norm. You will have an organisation where many people will have a very holistic view of things, because these double-hat people (and the more the better) will need to see things from different perspectives all the time. They need to (learn to) understand the contradictions and competitions and manage the conflicts between different interests.

These are some examples of 'pairs' that have worked for me in the past in my client work:

■ Country head and pan-European brand manager
■ Local Finance Controller *also* responsible for a small cost centre

- Head of IT *and* chair of a Sales-related committee
- Head of Customer Relationship Management (CRM) in country X *and* CRM manager leading the pan-European implementation of a new system
- Head of HR *and* sponsor of competitor intelligence task force

How can you implement double hats? Assign competing or parallel responsibilities. This is not a simple division of the cake or a justification for doing two jobs for the price of one. At senior level, make double hats a requirement. Watching a key competitor and having broader managerial responsibilities at the same time works very well for them! The examples above are ones of 'big roles'. The same applies to smaller roles within the firm, at middle management level or below. With junior people start with small but real role rotations first and then assign true double hats.

It is not uncommon in large corporations to see people who have several reporting lines. Reporting to both the country manager and the head of the global function (Finance, for example) is a typical example. The main reason for this is control. The command and control philosophy requires that everybody has a clear idea of who the boss is. The invention of the different kinds of reporting lines ('solid', 'dotted', etc.) was a way to weight those reporting 'loyalties'. You may know some people who have these double reporting lines. And you may also know that many of them see it as a real pain. I would like you to view double reporting lines as an opportunity to have multiple points of influence, of knowledge about what's going on, of corporate connections. If you ignore the command and control mode, the double reporting line is actually a true contrarian blessing. A double reporting line and double hats may or may not go together. People with double hats may in fact report to a single boss. But the principle is similar: divide loyalties, wear different pairs of spectacles, feel the tensions and contradictions and navigate through them. The disruptive idea is to thrive on those tensions and contradictions, not to avoid them. The accelerated learning you go through will pay off. Not just for you, but also for the organisation.

WEAR SEVERAL HATS INSIDE THE ORGANISATION, JUST LIKE YOU PROBABLY DO OUTSIDE THE FIRM.

NEVER ACCEPT ONE ROLE ONLY.

SEEK TO MANAGE TWO COMPETITIVE ANGLES OF THE FIRM SIMULTANEOUSLY.

TWO REPORTING LINES IS BAD. THREE IS MUCH BETTER. THE MORE BOSSES, THE BETTER FOR ALMOST EVERYTHING, INCLUDING SPEED OF LEARNING AND EXPERIENCE.

MAKE YOUR PEOPLE FEEL THE TENSION OF 'DIVIDED LOYALTIES': COLLECTIVE WHINGING TIME WILL DECREASE DRAMATICALLY.

Structures

Your own ideas/plans

....
....
....
....
....
....
....
....
....
....
....
....
....
....
....
....
....
....
....
....

Imagine...

Imagine that most managers in your organisation are able to see business life from different perspectives or competing angles most of the time. This creates a culture of broad and holistic views where people are sensitive to each other's jobs and responsibilities and where people are able to 'wear others' shoes'. In this culture, allocation of finite resources is far less painful and silos more difficult to create. This simple double hat 'structure' has the potential not only to enhance people's learning, but also to create a sense of 'commons' where internal collaboration rules over internal competition. Imagine the kind of behaviours that are visible in the organisation when double hats are the norm. What does that culture look and feel like? Imagine how you can start injecting those behaviours by modifying this 'structural rule' and trying double hats. Make a list of pairs (Mr Competitor X and head of country A; Mr Head of global IT and sponsor of implementation of an IT project for a particular market, etc.).

In your organisation

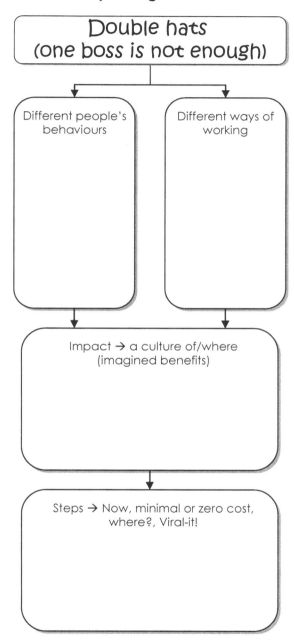

Double hats
(one boss is not enough)

Different people's behaviours

Different ways of working

Impact → a culture of/where (imagined benefits)

Steps → Now, minimal or zero cost, where?, Viral-it!

Structures 3	

Shadow jobs

In our **Western management system we are used to one person, one job, one box on the organisation chart. Duplications are thought to be a waste. But shadowing somebody in their job (and having a buddy) may actually be far from a luxury.**

Certainly, the larger the firm, the greater the chances that people are being boxed in by a particular 'job description'. It is part of our business 'efficiency' and 'focus'. The alternative would be called duplication or waste. But we have taken this box too far, because when the employee leaves, he takes the content of the box (his knowledge, experience and expertise) with him, leaving nothing but an empty container on the organisation chart.

There are other approaches – mainly, but not only, Japanese – where the idea of overlapping boxes and some degree of 'duplication' is not only acceptable, but the norm. It makes sense from a learning perspective. In reality, shadowing others in their job is far from being a waste or duplication or lack of focus. It's actually more like a way of preserving organisational memory and creating knowledge transfer. The shadower does not have to have 100% of the other person's knowledge or be a carbon copy. He just has to have a good enough understanding of what is going on, so he's able to jump in if needed, whether partially or totally.

Through shadowing, knowledge gets spread and extra expertise is created. It may be a bit counterintuitive when you implement it for the first time, particularly if you pay too much attention to the 'Focus Police', who will be horrified. But it will pay off. Like any other of these 10+10+10 disruptive ideas, this one has the potential to transform the organisation into a true knowledge sharing one, where the risk of losing corporate I.Q is minimised.

Shadowing works well, not only between closely related jobholders (project leader A and project leader B), but also between more distant 'relatives'. The greater the distance, the more counterintuitive it will feel and the more horrified the 'Focus Police' will be, but if you are brave enough to push through, you will see the benefits in the knowledge sharing arena. I am not suggesting you go crazy and come up with impossible shadowing pairs, but you need to give some thought to how far you want to go.

Shadowing should not confuse people, particularly if it is a fairly widespread practice and accountabilities are clear. One of the other 10+10+10 processes suggests that you obsessively fix accountability and worry less about everything else! The shadower doesn't share any responsibility with the person he shadows and that has to be made clear.

A cousin of shadowing is the buddy system, but there are differences. A buddy is somebody else in the organisation who you have frequent conversations with and with whom you share ideas, questions, answers or simply impressions of what is going on, what's working or not, etc. Strictly speaking, the buddies are not shadowing each other's jobs; they are simply sharing experiences from different parts of the organisation in a sort of corporate friendship. Whilst management can organise shadowing as a practice, it can hardly dictate a buddy system, but my advice is that it should be encouraged.

Many people do their jobs in some degree of isolation, without having a good sense of what happens in other people's shoes. A buddy can open the windows and let some fantastic light in. Some buddy systems that have worked for me in my client work are:

- Sales people - HQ people
- Sales people, geography A - sales people geography B
- R&D - Marketing
- Legal - HR
- Legal - customer facing staff
- HQ people - any non-HQ people

Shadowing and buddies should not be confused with mentoring either. A mentor has a clear remit in facilitating the mentored learning, whether in specific business skills or in leadership. Although a buddy can theoretically be a bit of a mentor, this is not his primary objective. In shadowing you can, of course, also see some elements of mentoring, but, again, this is not the main focus.

Implementing shadowing

- You could start in the obvious areas with high knowledge transfer potential; areas where the jobholders are closely related, such as project leaders in the Product Development division or sales managers in different sectors or lines of products. Then it could spread virally to other parts of the company by reinforcing the benefits. Tip: have product leaders spread stories about the benefits of shadowing both for themselves and the organisation.
- Make shadowing a specific part of people's objectives and therefore part of their performance appraisal. It implies that you will factor in a minimum amount of slack into the system. It is difficult to shadow someone else when you can hardly cope with your own job. But just think of the liability of losing two people who could not cope with their jobs and who didn't transfer any

knowledge to anybody else because they didn't have any means to do it!

- Have a mechanism in place to check how the shadowing is working, for example by gently (or not so gently) asking the shadower to report on a particular issue encountered.

- Encourage a buddy system particularly between HQ and non-HQ people and between sales people in different territories.

INCLUDE SHADOWING SOMEBODY IN A DIFFERENT ROLE IN EVERY JOB DESCRIPTION.

MAKE 'THE PAIR' THE UNIT OF KNOWLEDGE MANAGEMENT OR SIMPLY 'THE UNIT OF WORK'. (IT WORKS FOR COPS AND IT WILL WORK FOR YOU.)

THERE WILL BE DOZENS OF ARGUMENTS AGAINST IT, INCLUDING WASTE AND LACK OF FOCUS. RESIST THEM IF YOU WANT TO LEARN AT TWICE THE SPEED.

AN ORGANISATION THAT HAS SHADOWING BY DESIGN IS SUPER-RICH. KNOWLEDGE IS THE ONLY ASSET THAT MULTIPLIES ITSELF WHEN DIVIDED.

Your own ideas/plans

....
....
....
....
....
....
....
....
....
....
....
....
....
....
....
....
....
....
....
....

Imagine...

Imagine that shadowing is a common practice amongst some jobs or layers of management or sectors of the company. Imagine that your organisation can comfortably afford the fact that some people leave or are drawn into urgent projects (imagine a due diligence for an acquisition) without having to panic about gaps in knowledge and expertise. Imagine that the culture of the organisation is one of systematic knowledge transfer and learning, with shadowing as a key ingredient. First imagine the benefits and deal with 'the price to pay' (if any) later. Imagine that when somebody joins the company, shadowing is part of their job description from day one. Now imagine what will happen when you apply this across the board... Also, imagine the image your organisation will project to the outside world.

In your organisation

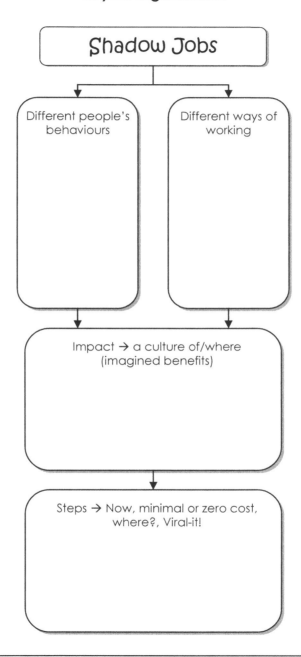

Shadow Jobs

Different people's behaviours

Different ways of working

Impact → a culture of/where (imagined benefits)

Steps → Now, minimal or zero cost, where?, Viral-it!

Structures 4 # Everything a project

Projects, big or small, have objectives, a beginning and end, allocated resources, accountable people, timelines and a budget. If you are doing anything in your organisation that doesn't qualify as a project, chances are it is redundant.

'Everything is a project' is a powerful philosophy. It injects discipline into what we do. If you work in an organisation that has 'projects' and 'other things' (not called projects), you may be at risk of having two separate worlds with different standards. When we say Joe works on a project or is a member of project X, we usually mean that he is part of a group that has objectives, timelines, milestones and resources. We understand that.

When HR manager Mary needs to hire 3 new people, we don't call this a project and don't see it the same way as Joe's work on the project team. Why? We see this as Mary just doing what she is supposed to do. But there is no difference between Joe and Mary. Both tasks should be a project. If this is already obvious to you, congratulations!

But before you sing the 'what's all the fuss about' song, take a look at your organisation and see if this really is the norm. This is one of the many trivial-looking things that are easy to dismiss. If you are a manager, can you tell yourself - with your hand on your heart - that everything in your department has the discipline of a project? Just by doing the exercise you may actually find that there are many things that perhaps still do not fit. If this is the case, I suggest you 'projectise' everything that moves...

For a long time, I have been using our 'Project Anatomy™' model to dissect activities and see how the ingredients of the project work. This is not only a useful exercise to understand projects, but also to convert 'other things' into a project with the consequent discipline. These are the components of 'Project Anatomy™':

- **Planning:** is there any? Most 'declared' or labelled projects would have some planning, but other 'activities' may not. Inject it everywhere. What does it look like?
- **Decision making:** who decides what, when, how? And, equally important, who does not make decisions? Ask people to think ahead, days or even months and see if they can answer the question, "*who will make a decision when we reach that point?*"

- **Resource allocation:** where are the resources? How are they managed? Think beyond money. Think time and people, perhaps even people that do not report to you.

- **Priority system**: is there one? How do things move up and down on the priority list? In many cases, prioritisation means things only go up, never down! Do you know the trade-offs?

- **Accountability:** who is doing what and who is not? Where does the buck stop? Accountability can't be shared. Responsibilities can. Who is ultimately going to be 'taken to account'?

- **Reporting:** how do we know we are on track and who needs to know? Could you have a snapshot of what is going on as frequently as you want to?

- **Knowledge transfer:** is there a mechanism to share the learning or is everything staying in people's heads?

The above is a simple framework to launch or monitor projects, or to convert 'other activities' into projects. It does not try to replace a project management system! Project management is a state of mind, not a piece of software or a method. When I say, "*everything is a project*", I am referring to a philosophy, a mentality, an attitude towards work and organisation, not to the creation of bar and Gann charts for everything. Those may help to visualise and discuss, but their existence does not ensure a 'project management mentality' per se.

Examples of projects, other than the ones we see naturally in Product Development, are:

- Hiring somebody
- An induction programme for somebody joining the organisation
- A company conference or convention
- Exploring the benefits of a new software and finding a vendor
- Finding new premises
- Finding an external consultant
- Rolling out a financial plan
- Making division A and division B talk to each other
- Review all salaries
- Persuading John of the merits of X
- Get the Board to approve B

You will notice that some of the above resonate easily as projects, whilst others - such as 'get the Board to approve B' - don't naturally come to mind as such. And *that* is the issue! Your goal should be: 100% of all activities around me are projects, i.e. feel like projects, behave as projects and are treated as projects. So, what can you do?

Look around and ask: "*Is this a project?*" If not, what is it? Should you do it? Don't dismiss this exercise too quickly. All the 10+10+10=1000 practices are relatively simple on their own. Let's say that you are already converted to the project philosophy (everything has objectives, beginning and end, allocated resources, accountable people, timelines and a budget), but:

- your colleagues or subordinates may not be and you have never had a proper conversation with them on this topic.
- you may discover that the 'non-project' activity surpasses the project activity. If this is the case, I think you are in trouble.
- you may find people saying, *"We don't have time to run projects, we have jobs to do."* And if this is the case, you are in trouble as well.

PROJECTISE EVERYTHING.

CALL IT A PROJECT. WE ARE ALL PROJECTS.
(MY COMPANY IS A PROJECT.)

IF IT ISN'T A PROJECT, WHAT IS IT?

IF IT ISN'T A PROJECT, IT SHOULDN'T HAVE
A BUDGET (WORKS WONDERS TO FOCUS
MINDS).

'DOING STUFF' AND 'BUSY-NESS' ARE NOT
SYNONYMOUS WITH PROJECTS.

MARKET YOURSELF ON YOUR ABILITY TO
RUN PROJECTS.

Structures

Your own ideas/plans

....

....

....

....

....

....

....

....

....

....

....

....

....

....

....

....

....

....

....

....

Imagine...

Imagine that all the activities in the organisation are treated with the discipline of a project. Picture life in your organisation and imagine the kind of culture this creates. One where people don't feel that there are pockets of waste or that they are doing things of unclear value... A culture of discipline in understanding why you are doing things and how to execute them. A culture where activities can't hide behind the smokescreen of 'too many processes' or 'systems', because the objectives, the declared beginning and end, the desired outcome and the plan to get there are all clear and transparent. Imagine that you can label 100% of your activities - your own or the ones you manage - as a project, big or small.

In your organisation

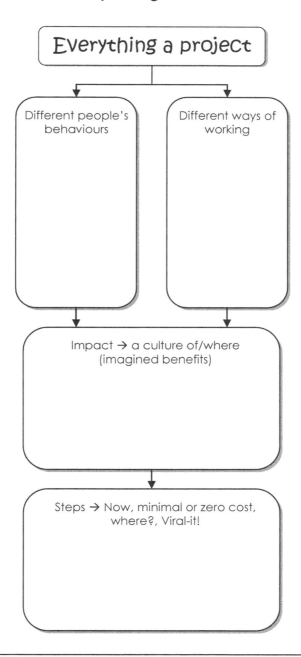

Structures 5

Management by invitation

Corporate grade, reporting lines and membership of leadership teams in organisations often go together. But unbundling these components is a healthy exercise and a powerful rule in the maths of change.

If you report to Joe - CEO, divisional director or country manager - chances are you share this with another eight or ten people who constitute Joe's management team, executive committee or leadership team. This is what the organisation chart says. Most management teams are formed by what the organisation chart dictates; by an 'accidental' reporting line. Everybody reporting to Joe is de facto a member of his management team.

In medium-sized or large corporations, structures are very often cross- or multi-functional. Imagine a Business Unit composed of a large Sales function, a smaller Marketing function and then a series of support functions such as HR, Finance, Legal, IT and perhaps a very small Strategy Team. The leadership team of that Unit is bound to be composed of the Director of Sales, the Director of Marketing, the Finance Controller, Legal counsel, the Head of IT and the Head of the Strategy Team. I suggest that this happened by default, by the dictation of the organisation chart and that nobody ever questioned it.

But a legitimate question may be, "*does everybody need to be part of that leadership team?*" Many people in business organisations would of course say 'no'. But the way we sometimes solve the issue is by promotion/demotion. For example, we may say only directors are really part of the management team. This is managing by grade, not by brain and it's not what I am suggesting. Grade in the corporate structure (VP, director, manager, head) should not be a criterion of membership of a particular leadership team. Membership should be by invitation only. And only those who are in a capacity to add value to the role - whether they are in charge of a large part of the cake or not – should be invited.

It may be that, on reflection, the leadership team of the above Business Unit example should be composed of the Director of Marketing, the Director of Sales, the Head of HR and two country managers who do not report directly to the top leader of the Business Unit, but who are called upon to serve on that leadership team.

There may be alternative arrangements, but the principle is one of 'by invitation only'. A principle that forces you to stop taking for granted the fact that membership will happen automatically or that grade or rank are a form of entitlement. It may be counterintuitive at first, but it is very effective. Much of the counterintuitive aspect comes from the fact that we tend to have pre-conceived ideas about how the organisation should work. Sometimes these ideas carry flawed assumptions:

- We must be inclusive. Yes, I agree but it is inclusiveness by invitation. If people feel the need to have all the direct reports together from time to time or, indeed, on a regular basis, they could have some sort of 'Staff Committee' (of all direct reports) if there were reasons for them to meet. But Staff Committee is not the same as a leadership team.

- We must be fair. That assumes that all reporting lines to Joe are equal. In the above example it may have been considered unfair to the Financial Controller not to include him in the leadership team. There is nothing unfair about a selection made on transparent grounds. Inclusiveness and so-called fairness sometimes result in gross unfairness to the group, because the artificial composition makes the team ineffective or highly unbalanced.

- We must be democratic. Democracy is a form of government, not a type of organisation (unless you work for a company that ballots everybody to elect a CEO!).

When you question management team compositions for the first time and, de facto, try to unbundle corporate grades, leadership and reporting lines, you will encounter some negative reactions and a few puzzled faces. But once this has been accepted as a legitimate questioning of the status quo, a breeze of healthy fresh air will start to flow through your organisation!

Something that you may want to try as a model to follow is the Board of Directors. Though there are some differences between countries, a Board of Directors in public companies is usually composed of a few executives and some non-executive directors, who are either representing some shareholder sector or participating as members on their own capacity, background, experience or particular expertise. We have accepted this kind of designed composition as normal when it comes to the Board, but this is far from common for executive and leadership committees. But there is no reason why you could not mirror this, unless you want to stick to the default position because, *"we have never done it like that."*

UNBUNDLE REPORTING LINES AND THE
MANAGEMENT TEAM.

NOT EVERYBODY WHO REPORTS TO YOU
SHOULD BE ON YOUR MANAGEMENT TEAM.
NOT EVERYBODY WHO IS ON YOUR
MANAGEMENT TEAM SHOULD REPORT TO
YOU.

'BOSS' AND 'SUBORDINATE' CAN SIT
TOGETHER AT A THIRD PARTY
MANAGEMENT TEAM. SO FAR, THERE IS NO
LAW TO PROHIBIT THIS!

INCLUDE EXECS AND NON-EXECS IN YOUR
MANAGEMENT TEAM AS IF IT WERE A
COMPANY'S BOARD OF DIRECTORS.

Your own ideas/plans

....
....
....
....
....
....
....
....
....
....
....
....
....
....
....
....
....
....
....
....

Imagine...

Imagine a culture where membership of leadership teams at different levels is not automatic as a result of the organisation chart. Imagine a culture where that kind of membership is by invitation only and the composition of many management teams reflects that. This is a culture where (1) corporate grades, (2) reporting lines and (3) leadership are unbundled and where people are asking questions about who should be on leading teams. In this culture, leadership teams follow a 'Board of Directors' model and are rich and diverse in composition. Imagine how you can start implementing this on a small scale, Who do you invite? Imagine the healthy conversations you may need to have about stereotypical concepts such as 'unfairness' and 'democratic'!

In your organisation

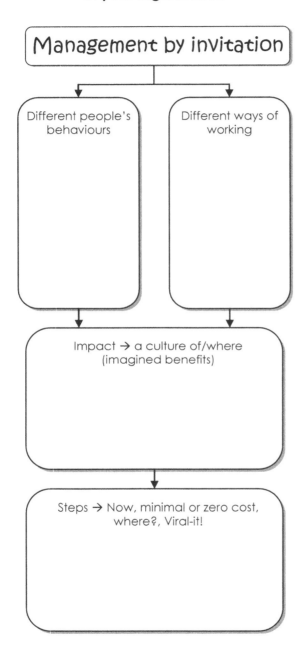

Management by invitation

Different people's behaviours

Different ways of working

Impact → a culture of/where (imagined benefits)

Steps → Now, minimal or zero cost, where?, Viral-it!

Structures 6 # Fixed-term teams

Teams' lifecycles should be designed with fixed-term membership and an automatic review, so that healthy questioning of their existence occurs on a regular basis. And this review should be more than a simple review. It is a beginning, an end... and a new beginning. Create, disband and recreate teams, but never give them an unlimited life span.

To fix a term for teams and their membership sounds like yet another 'obvious' thing to do, but the reality is that in many cases teams seem to have a life of their own and tend to drag on well beyond their 'sell-by date'. It should be a simple discipline to design a beginning and an end for teams, with their goals, objectives and milestones mapped out in between. But I would not fix the end to coincide with the moment when *everything* has been achieved, but around the achievement of milestones. Fixing terms will focus people's minds on what needs to be achieved and will help achieve it in a 'shorter' period of time. The team's membership can even be totally or partially modified or upgraded within the total life of the team. Some people would say, *"Yes, of course."* However, for each team disbandment or simple existence query, there are hundreds of team formations. We are very good at formation, but not so good at declaring that the mission has been accomplished or a key milestone achieved and that a new team should take over.

I am stretching the argument here, because I know that in some cases the membership of the 'new' team may be very similar to the 'old' one. But this is not the issue. It should be a matter of principle that the new team is launched, if need be, the day after the previous team has been 'disbanded'. This fixed-term life has the advantage of reminding everybody of the fact that things won't be allowed to simply drag on with peaks of excitement and periods of silence. It forces the different functions providing members to a cross-functional team to re-think their presence, the value of their contributions and to decide on the best people to join and serve in those teams.

Examples of these fixed-term teams that have worked well in my consulting work are:

- Interdisciplinary brand marketing teams that are formed to prepare a business plan, strategic plan or annual cycle and are disbanded as soon as the budget has been approved. The next team is in charge of the implementation of the strategy and may or may not have the same cross-disciplinary members.

■ Product development teams that focus on reaching a particular milestone and that are disbanded when they reach it, only to be re-created immediately for the next phase. Whether the project leader is the same or not, is irrelevant. The declaration of the 'end' is a terribly symbolic thing to do, as is the declaration of a new beginning. It also punctuates the fact that the time has come to get new membership applications.

Some people may call this just a game, but organisational life is full of games and rituals and this one adds many benefits such as:

■ continuous focus on outcomes

■ guaranteed review of membership

■ guaranteed assessment of effectiveness

■ provision to change leadership to one more appropriate to the phase

To some extent, fixed-term teams are the equivalent of parking spaces that are signposted '2 hour maximum, no return within 1 hour'. The notice is very clear: this is as long as you can stay and once you have left, you can't come back within the hour to give a chance to others to park. Even the second part could apply to teams, although there may be cases where that may not be realistic.

> ALL TEAMS HAVE A CLAUSE IN THEIR
> MISSION STATEMENTS: THIS TEAM WILL BE
> DISBANDED, NO MATTER WHAT, BY
> MIDNIGHT (DATE HERE).
>
> PUBLICISE INTERNAL TEAM FORMATIONS
> AND TEAM DISCHARGES HEAVILY.
>
> CONSIDER SOME FUNCTIONS OR TEAM
> MEMBERSHIPS AS 'MAY NOT RETURN
> WITHIN SIX MONTHS'.

Your own ideas/plans

....
....
....
....
....
....
....
....
....
....
....
....
....
....
....
....
....
....
....
....

Imagine...

Imagine that your organisation has a continuous creation and disbandment of teams with no team continuing past the end of its life cycle. Imagine that all team members have a clear idea of the beginning and end of the team, of the fixed term. Imagine that in everybody's mind the following question is present at the start: *"What am I going to leave behind when the team ceases to exist on that fixed end day?"* What kind of different behaviours will you see? What kind of culture will you be creating? What will be the benefits? Imagine the compound effect of many teams working in fixed-term mode. Perhaps you can start or experiment with part of the organisation. Imagine how you can do that and then spread the rule to other parts.

In your organisation

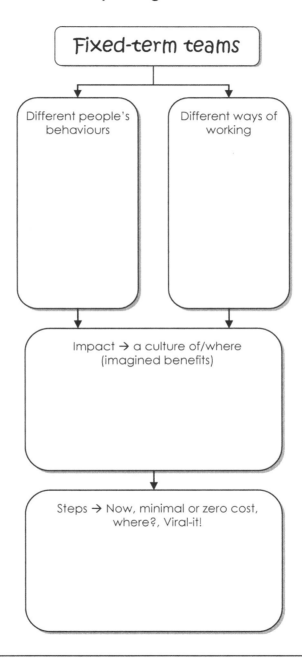

Fixed-term teams

Different people's behaviours

Different ways of working

Impact → a culture of/where (imagined benefits)

Steps → Now, minimal or zero cost, where?, Viral-it!

98

Structures 7	# Net-work, not more teamwork

Organisations have become proficient in team management and teams have become the natural structure for collaboration, the default position. But in these days of inter-dependence between roles and jobs, many collaboration solutions can be found in informal networks, not in designed, cohesive teams.

Let me inject another contrarian idea: you don't need any more teams. I know, I know, *teamocracies* rule the waves. We all talk about teams and how to make them stronger, more effective, etc. Teams are at the centre of organisational development and somehow we have equated them to 'collaboration' or people working together.

Teams are here to stay and I'm not going to waste any more space justifying their existence. But what we really need to do is not to refine the team machinery, but to exploit the net-work one. The organisation is composed of a number of collaborative spaces. Some of them are relatively rigid and designed - teams, task forces - while others are composed of looser connections between individuals, with different degrees and nuances of the word 'looser'. Some communities (of practice or interest) are semi-loose, with a more or less defined membership. There are other networks of connections of a much looser nature, represented by people who sometimes know very little about each other and/or only communicate from time to time. There is a wide spectrum of connections available, but traditional management has only focused on one end; the one where structures are designed and borders given: the teams.

In recent years, people of different disciplines interested in organisational life have begun to suspect that the structure of teams may not be as universally desirable as we first thought, particularly when the organisation needs to tap into intellectual capital wherever it is. We need more and more people who are able to navigate, to ride the looser informal connections where many answers to innovation lie. Teams are too predictable in their capability to answer questions such as, *"is there a different way?"* Even if the answer is yes, chances are 'that way' is to be found within the confines of the team.

We need to favour looser network structures, even if we won't have the same command and control capacity as we do with teams and taskforces. This is the price to pay. It is from those sometimes un-structured conversations that true innovation originates; it is there that many answers to questions can be found. What can you do?

- For starters, don't oppose people spending some time networking inside the firm. If you have a formal IT system for that, you are well advanced. Many organisations are just beginning to come to terms with the idea that people are connecting and will continue to connect routinely outside the boundaries of the division, team or department. But is this not something that even traditional management wanted to do?

- Promote the idea that people should go 'outside' for questions and answers. 'Outside' may just mean inside the company, but in another division or affiliate. People should pick up the phone and be able to ask a colleague miles away, perhaps somebody they have never even met, how they solved problem A. Going beyond the natural boundaries should be the norm, not the exception. These are not behaviours reserved for one-off situations or annual internal company conventions, where so-called Best Practices are shared. This is not enough. We need real time sharing of those best practices or best ideas.

- We simply need the ability for somebody in sales in the South of the country to be able to shout, *"Houston, we have a problem"* and then get help/an answer almost on the spot, because he is reaching an entire network of potential experts for solving the problem. Not just his peers, not just his immediate team, not just his boss. And frankly, if you think this can be done via email, forget it.

You need to accept that it is much messier than organisation chart management and a command-and-control style of leadership, but you can no longer afford people on the payroll who are *only* good at the internal dynamics of the team. Chances are you have lots of those already. You need net-working as a routine process and this is different from the standard networking: something that usually has the emphasis on the net, not the work.

Teams are predictable structures. They are very good for operational delivery, but not so good for strategy or innovation. A certain degree of 'groupthink' is always present. Putting the net-work before the teamwork ensures the continuous flow of new ideas. If the old saying *"If you have two people who think the same, fire one of them!"* were to be applied to teams, the world population of teams would shrink by 50%.

MEASURE PEOPLE'S NET-WORK WEALTH BY THE NUMBER OF THEIR CONNECTIONS (WEAK OR STRONG) WITH OTHERS, INSIDE AND OUTSIDE THE BOUNDARIES OF THE COMPANY.

MEASURE YOUR OWN NET-WORK WEALTH BY THE NUMBER OF PEOPLE YOU COULD CALL FOR HELP IN THE MIDDLE OF THE NIGHT …

MAKE SOCIAL CONNECTIVITY (OUTSIDE TEAMS) A KEY FEATURE OF THE CULTURE.

EVERYBODY SHOULD ROUTINELY CROSS THE BORDER OF THEIR DIVISIONS, GROUPS OR TEAMS IN PURSUIT OF ANSWERS OR TO DELIVER INPUT.

ASK THE FOLLOWING PERFORMANCE MANAGEMENT QUESTIONS ROUTINELY: HOW MANY PEOPLE OUTSIDE THIS (TEAM, DIVISION, COMPANY) HAVE YOU TALKED TO IN THE LAST MONTH? HOW MANY PIECES OF INPUT HAVE YOU GIVEN TO PEOPLE OUTSIDE YOUR DEPARTMENT?

104

Your own ideas/plans

....
....
....
....
....
....
....
....
....
....
....
....
....
....
....
....
....
....
....
....

Imagine...

Imagine that people in your organisation are always using networks of connections with colleagues - some of them remote - in order to find new ideas, solutions, to ask for help, etc. Imagine a culture of fluid communication between people in different divisions or groups, well beyond the inter-team communication or the so-called cross-functional teams. Imagine that cross-functionality is a constant feature of daily work, not something only reserved for the cyclical meeting of teams. A culture where net-working is promoted or rewarded; where the wealth of connections, including informal and loose, is the true measure of the value of your human and social capital. What does that culture look like? What will be different from your status quo?

In your organisation

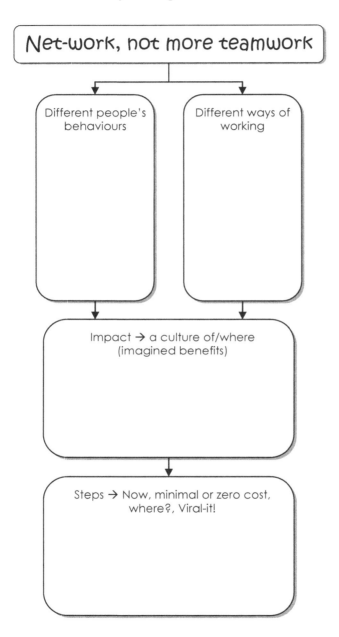

Structures 8

Support functions are businesses ('market tested')

Support functions such as HR, Finance or IT should survive the market test. Could they become self-contained businesses with their own portfolio of clients? If the answer is no, chances are you could outsource all of them. If the answer is yes, don't let them go.

A while ago, a friend of mine - running an R&D Strategy Department and sitting on the Board of one of the largest companies in the world - confessed to me that there were two kinds of people at that Board: the ones with profit and loss (P&L) responsibilities and the ones without. In other words, the ones who brought in money and the ones who spent it...like himself. It was clear to him that despite his glorious title and the undoubted importance of his role he was just a second-class citizen. You can find this pattern in many organisations. Everybody in a management committee or leadership team is equal, but some are more equal than others.

A division with Marketing and Sales that has dedicated support from Finance, HR, Product Development, perhaps Legal, etc., is bound to have all those functions represented at its leadership team. However, meetings may be spent solely discussing sales forecasts and brand plans with everybody else switching off. Sometimes, some of the so-called 'support functions' only seem to be at meetings to create an audience. Even when there are items allocated to talent retention, an HR topic, everybody knows that what *really* matters are those sales figures!

Am I drawing a caricature? You may be lucky and have a different experience; one where your HR, Finance, IT, etc. are real and equal partners to Marketing and Sales. Congratulations. But if this is not the case, you have two options:

- Leave it as it is and acknowledge that you have first and second-class citizens.
- Create support functions that feel, smell, behave, plan and act as businesses, not as servants taking orders.

So-called support functions, usually those mentioned above, are often in need of a big overhaul. A management team that has managed to have truly equal members, whether they represent income generating functions or not, is a mature management team. There are a few problems on this journey, however. Your support functions - or their leaders - may not be ready or up to the challenge. They may be in theory, but not in reality. Examples are:

- HR functions that are biased towards the hiring/firing of people, but with poor insight into organisational development.
- Finance functions that are good at crunching numbers, controlling costs and managing spreadsheets, but that have no real strategic insight.
- Legal functions that tell you what you cannot do, but that can't create alternative scenarios.

It is your choice to create one, two or three classes of citizens, but any dichotomy of the 'core – non-core' type is risky business.

The aim of any 'support function' should be to become so good, that they are able to become a quasi independent business unit within the firm (with P&L, if argument stretched). One of the tests to determine this is the market test. Could that function be totally outsourced and provide better 'support' to you? If the answer is yes, you - head of the function - have a problem: you are disposable. If the answer is no, then you are heading a first-class citizen function: you are better than what the market can provide. I am not suggesting you take the outsourcing route for the sake of following a trend, but as a test. And I am not talking about cost either. You could outsource everything (including your thinking, if somebody else did it for you. And believe me, I know many people who seem to have done just that) and perhaps cut costs, but that doesn't make it a good strategy. However, the discipline of the test is very healthy.

In my experience, there are four stages in the progression from second-class citizen support function (disposable) to first-class business unit (of any description):

- **Silent witness.** They are 'there' and 'do things', but they seem to be on another planet unless they occasionally show up with specific, standard and predictable deliveries appropriate to their roles.
- **Servility.** They are more than silent witnesses, but they just seem to take orders and comply with requests if they can. In my opinion, the customer-centrism mantra has gone awfully wrong when it's translated like this into internal relationships. Incredibly foolish ideas such as 'the customer is always right' have created an internal illusion of service, where first-class citizens (P&L people) are being served by second-class citizens (support functions). We have de facto created a generation of second-class reactive people.
- **Partnership.** There is true equality between functions and both strategy creation and execution are joint efforts. This model requires a level of maturity (experience, confidence, credibility) in those support functions and the

existence of this maturity is not always obvious to me when working with my client organisations.

■ **Partnership, market tested.** As mentioned above, the function could theoretically walk out and be a business on its own merit. This may be counterintuitive or simply contrarian. There may be many people reluctant to go that route. Sure, but you could start small and have one of those functions 'tested by the market'. You could even start it as a feasibility project/game, with lots of reassurance to people that there are no plans to get rid of the function! The better they are and the greater the possibilities of the function walking out 'as a business', the more you should want to keep them!

DEFINE 'CUSTOMER' AS SOMEONE EXTERNAL TO THE COMPANY. FOR EACH MINUTE SPENT PLAYING THE GAME 'YOU ARE MY CUSTOMER, I AM YOUR CUSTOMER' INTERNALLY, A REAL CUSTOMER WALKS OUT.

IF A CUSTOMER INITIATIVE IS NOT A JOINT MARKETING-SALES-IT-HR-FINANCE-LEGAL EFFORT, CHANCES ARE SUPPORTING FUNCTIONS ARE TAKING A BACK SEAT AND DON'T CONSIDER THEMSELVES AS 'THE BUSINESS' (AND IF THEY'RE NOT, WHY SHOULD THEY BE ON THE PAYROLL?).

AFTER FIELD/CUSTOMER VISITS ARE COMPLETED BY SUPPORT FUNCTIONS, THEY SHOULD DO SOMETHING DIFFERENT IN REPORTING BACK TO HQ.

MARKET-TEST SUPPORT FUNCTIONS ANNUALLY.

Your own ideas/plans

....

....

....

....

....

....

....

....

....

....

....

....

....

....

....

....

....

....

....

Imagine...

Imagine that people in IT, Finance, Legal or HR for example are undistinguishable from those in Sales, Marketing or Product development in their ability to understand the business and live it fully. Imagine that you can truly put your hand on your heart and say that there are no second-class citizens in your management team. How far do you like to go? Imagine a culture where all the 'functions' are true partners, where customer focus is a true joint effort. What does that organisation look like? Imagine the kind of HR, or Finance or IT or Legal you would like to have. Imagine that they all live 'the business itself', not just the support to the business. What kind of behaviours do you think will be different? What will you see? And do you want to inject those behaviours into your organisation? Imagine that all your support functions have a 'market test' every year. And that they are asked to report back on their standing versus what the external market could offer. Cost being only one of the considerations.

In your organisation

Support functions are businesses

Different people's
behaviours

Different ways of
working

Impact → a culture of/where
(imagined benefits)

Steps → Now, minimal or zero cost,
where?, Viral-it!

116

Structures 9   # Membership bids

Inviting bids from your own internal market for the membership of a project or team will create a culture where these membership decisions are assessed on their own merits and not in a 'management by default' mode. The consequences are significant.

Life in an organisation comes with a set of rules and expectations. On the expectation side, many are tacit: which teams to serve in, which training courses to attend, which committees to be part of, which reporting lines to adhere to. Once the box on the organisation chart has been filled and allocated to somebody, the expectations run on automatic pilot.

It would be very helpful and healthy to unbundle those expectations and invite bids for membership from your internal market. Projects, task forces, committees, etc. should be open to bids from people wanting to join, as opposed to being 100% dictated by hierarchy or assumption, i.e. I am manager of A; the cross-functional project team X needs a representative from A; I am therefore the logical representative of A on that project team.

There is a lot of passivity in our organisations: people are told which teams to join, which meetings to attend, which personal development courses they should be part of, etc. Of course, it is part of management's responsibility to have a say in those things, but without this invitation for 'membership bids' things could be taken for granted with nobody questioning things. In other words, this rule is a form of vaccination against 'management by default'.

Directly opposite the membership by dictation (designed by management) is voluntarism. Many people in organisations have had bad experiences with simple voluntarism for many good reasons:

- It doesn't necessarily attract the right people.
- There are 'chronic volunteers' who sign up for just about anything.
- Some of them truly are helpful souls, but others just like joining things because they see themselves as indispensable.
- It gives a false sense of democratisation.
- It is a distraction.
- It is impossible. People should stick to their own jobs. Being able to volunteer simply means they have very little to do.

However, inviting bids for membership is not the same as voluntarism. It simply means opening up the membership to the internal market, with specific criteria associated with the bidding and providing some healthy internal competition. It is about the organisation acknowledging that there are finite resources or opportunities and that they have to be allocated in the most effective way. It is about signalling to all that only true merit makes you eligible for joining specific groups or tasks, including leadership teams.

Some of the activities, opportunities, structures or 'projects' that will work well for an internal bidding model are:

■ Bidding for limited available places for training courses or personal development programmes.
■ Membership of specific teams or task forces.
■ Temporary teams or groups assessing X and reporting back
■ Community of practice
■ Change champions in a change management programme

Running the internal market model in the organisation has obvious advantages. But, like any good idea, you could take it too far and create a social-Darwinian environment where everybody is constantly competing. This would be disastrous. The model could also create problems of its own, but, on balance, it is a healthier model than the one where either entitlement or assumption of entitlement is the norm.

I really believe that collaboration and not competition is the true competitive advantage, whether inside or outside the firm. Membership bidding has to strike a balance between two opposing things:

1. a collaborative environment where people are able to tap into any other available human capital, wherever it is in the organisation.

2. a culture of 'management by default', where many things are predictable and implemented without questioning.

CREATE AN OPEN INTERNAL MARKET FOR
PROJECT MEMBERSHIP. POST PROFILES.
LET PEOPLE APPLY.

MAKE APPLYING (FOR TEAM MEMBERSHIP,
COURSE PLACES, ETC.) EXTREMELY SIMPLE
AND UN-BUREAUCRATIC.

INTERVIEW WITH ONE SINGLE QUESTION:
DESCRIBE WHY THIS PROJECT CAN'T WORK
WITHOUT YOU; WHAT WOULD BE THE COST
OF NOT HAVING YOU IN (X)?

ALSO, YOU WANT A COMPANY OF PEOPLE
WHO ARE ALWAYS WANTED FOR TEAMS
AND PROJECTS. HIRE ACCORDINGLY.

DEAL WITH THE 'NEVER WANTED' PEOPLE
FORCEFULLY. THEY MAY BE VERY
VALUABLE, BUT MAY NOT KNOW HOW TO
MARKET THEMSELVES. (OR THEY MAY BE
REDUNDANT AND BETTER OFF SOMEWHERE
ELSE.)

Your own ideas/plans

....
....
....
....
....
....
....
....
....
....
....
....
....
....
....
....
....
....
....

Imagine...

Imagine that the culture of your organisation is one of systematic reflection on who the best person is to do anything. That 'managing by default' (carrying on as always) isn't the norm. That people need to apply to become a member of key groups. Imagine a culture where an internal market plays a strong part in allocating resources or memberships to teams and task forces. A culture where management doesn't systematically dictate all and where staff don't automatically assume that their position on the organisation chart or their rank will determine their exposure to projects, ideas, reviews or use of resources such as training and professional development. What are the key behaviours? What do you like to see differently? Can you start somewhere small and then spread it out to other areas? What kind of safeguards do you need to put in place to avoid social-Darwinism? How do you deal with people who 'never apply' or are 'never wanted'?

In your organisation

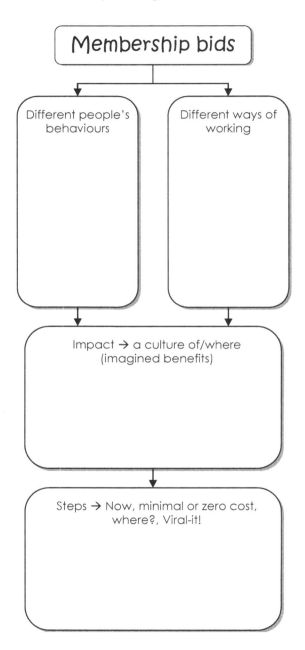

Membership bids

Different people's behaviours

Different ways of working

Impact → a culture of/where (imagined benefits)

Steps → Now, minimal or zero cost, where?, Viral-it!

Structures 10

Home effects

A powerful way of discovering how many homeless ideas or activities you have in your organisation is to simply ask the question, "*Where is 'home' for this initiative*?" People choose their loyalties and sense of belonging regardless of the organisation chart. Divided loyalties are good. Promote them. But for ideas or initiatives there must be a home somewhere.

Projects of any kind need a home, a place where they belong. This may sound trivial and just like another 'obvious thing'. However, in the organisation there are often many things that seem to be homeless. They don't really belong anywhere. And remember: belonging to too many places is just a different way of not belonging anywhere.

People in organisations tend to determine their own loyalties. There are people happy to belong to a global enterprise and its global objectives, but more frequently you will find that people are happier to belong to a particular project or to the endeavours of a particular country.

Some global disciplines are notorious for creating a sense of belonging to a sort of old 'guild. Information technology (IT) is one. People working in IT often say, *"I am in IT"* and only after that, *"I work for X"*. It is as if the discipline crosses the borders of companies and geographies. It may also be HR or another particular expertise. There is nothing intrinsically wrong with this, but you need to be very clear about where the sense of belonging is coming from in order to understand loyalty.

In large multinational companies there are often 'global teams' or 'global functions/disciplines'. It is very common to see business cards with the word 'Global' on the front: Global HR, Global R&D, Global Marketing, etc. This is very often nothing more than a statement of power, since in many cases it is usually obvious what the remit and scope are. When all the functions in HQ need to have a business card with the world 'Global' on it, you may wonder why they need to state it all the time...

The *globalisation* of the organisational life may be a more or less inevitable sign of the times and part of the nature of the modern firm, but very often it does nothing for people's sense of belonging to ideas, activities, objectives, etc. Globalisation by decree is not terribly smart if you are trying to embrace people who are really interested in the business of France or the business of brand

A. Globalisation is often imposed by HQ as a controlling and unifying mechanism with the hope that management will become simpler. But globalisation on paper doesn't necessarily mean than in reality hearts and minds are also global.

The smart approach to the building of 'home effects' would be to simply allow them. There may be one or more overlapping 'homes', but that doesn't mean that they are in conflict. And they will be in less conflict if you allow multiple senses of belonging without declaring it wrong or inconsistent with some sort of 'global vision'. In fact, you *want* those multiple homes! The disruptive part of this is that instead of wanting to homogenise things ('there is only one single Global Team') you will inject diversity.

The crucial points to remember about home effects are:

- Do I know what they are? Can I identify them in the people working with me/for me?
- Is there any conflict between those senses of belonging and what the company is aiming for? Are they compatible? Make them compatible!
- Suspending judgement and preconceived ideas, where are people's hearts and minds? The company? The project? The discipline? Me Inc? Me Ltd? Can I accommodate for those and still be OK?
- Are there things lost in the 'global space'? To appoint a global project leader does not

necessarily solve the problem. Sometimes it only provides an illusion of control.

- At a very local level, could all ongoing activities be linked to a particular home? Is this an HR project or an IT project or a brand marketing project? Again, the right answer does not come from simply looking at the names of the leaders or at the department letterhead.

Identifying homeless ideas and projects is crucial to determine the right level of energy and commitment. To adjudicate homes beyond the obvious dictation of the organisation chart is a simple mechanism to ensure healthy structures and working processes. Asking the question, *"Where is home for this?"* is a simple way of discovering disconnects and initiatives that may have started 'somewhere', but that now seem to continue with a life of their own. Providing 'the home effect' is one of the finest tasks for leaders.

In large organisations, many projects and initiatives are truly multidisciplinary and cross-functional. For them to work, they often need a high level 'sponsorship' from members of the top leadership team. This is usually a good mechanism to ensure 'home effects' beyond the functions, the divisions or the geographies. If the sponsor manages to act as a magnetic field, attracting commitment, energy and focus, he is de facto providing a home that caters for parallel senses of belonging. Starting with some projects is often a good way to spread this concept in a viral way.

PROVIDE IMMEDIATE PERMANENT SHELTER FOR HOMELESS IDEAS FLOATING AROUND THE ORGANISATION.

BAN THE WORD 'GLOBAL' UNLESS YOUR BUSINESS EMPIRE INCLUDES EVERYTHING FROM ALASKA TO ANDORRA. THE WORD IS PROBABLY UNNECESSARY AND IS EXTREMELY FRUSTRATING FOR THE NON-GLOBAL PEOPLE.

EVERYTHING MUST HAVE A HOME, SO CHECK FOR ACCOUNTABILITIES. SOMETHING THAT IS SHARED BY EVERYBODY (AS IN 'COLLECTIVE, SHARED RESPONSIBILITIES') IS PROBABLY HOMELESS.

NOT ONLY RESPECT DIFFERENT LOYALTIES, BUT PROMOTE THEM. DIVIDED LOYALTIES ARE GOOD. SINGLE LOYALTIES (BIG, I.E. 'GLOBAL' OR SMALL, I.E. 'MY BRAND') COME WITH TUNNEL VISION.

PEOPLE WITH ONLY ONE SINGLE LOYALTY ARE UNDER-QUALIFIED FOR THE ENTERPRISE.

130

Your own ideas/plans

....
....
....
....
....
....
....
....
....
....
....
....
....
....
....
....
....
....
....
....

Imagine...

Imagine that initiatives, projects or simply ideas in development always have a home in your organisation. Imagine a culture where homeless efforts are the anomaly; where people's loyalties and sense of belonging can be accommodated under different umbrellas. Imagine that you don't need to use the word 'global' all the time, because it feels redundant. Imagine the kind of behaviours that you will have and see in such a culture of well-crafted and cared-for loyalties. Imagine what will happen if you promote divided loyalties as a way to ensure richness of ideas and scope of people's vision. What difficulties will you encounter? How many politically correct positions ('there is only one global team'; 'there is only one single loyalty: to the company') will you have to fight? Imagine the benefits of the disruptive idea of embracing multiple, overlapping, sometimes conflicting loyalties full of opportunities!

In your organisation

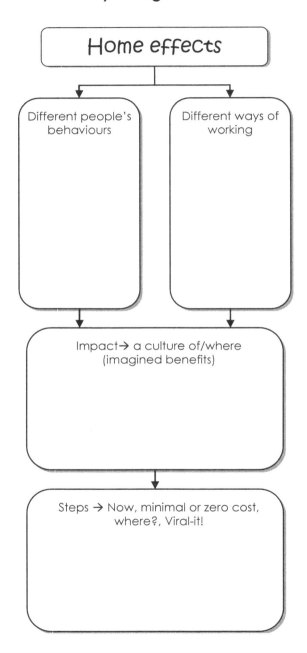

Home effects

Different people's behaviours

Different ways of working

Impact→ a culture of/where (imagined benefits)

Steps → Now, minimal or zero cost, where?, Viral-it!

Processes

Processes 1

Internal clocks

Organisational business life is rhythmical and cyclical with the clocks set externally to mark things such as 'quarters' and 'year end'. This tends to orchestrate internal cycles, but also creates straightjackets. You should create your own internal clocks, your own internal game.

There is nothing magical about a 365-day cycle, I know. It's called a year and it works for everybody. We also have seasons and a 24-hour night/day cycle. But 'the quarter' (3 months) is an invention of the stock market. It is an arbitrary unit of time that forces those in public companies to report (earnings, results in general, etc.) and orchestrates the internal rhythm of companies. The quarter is magical. It doesn't exist, but we behave as if it is *the* unit of time.

Also, think of the annual budget cycle. As a manager, you are rich on the 1st of January and you become progressively poorer as you get closer to the 31st of December, only to get rich again on the 1st of January.

Is that not a bit crazy? In some companies you will also be spending a lot of time on the so-called budget process 'for next year' (i.e. how rich you will be on the following 1st of January). And you are doing this whilst still spending the money of the current year.

What happens with new ideas, new initiatives, things that were 'not in the budget' or that you had 'no budget for'? You park them for assessment, for review in...the next budget cycle, usually next year, 365 days into the future! Of course there are exceptions and you may have the authority to re-allocate funds across the firm and make decisions on the spot for substantial reshuffling. But the average manager does not. The 365-day budget cycle doesn't make any sense in terms of making decisions rapidly, perhaps to react to market changes or innovation, to fund new ideas or to allow for agility to adapt as you go along. It is a very rigid framework and simply too long-term thinking. It suits the company's reporting obligations, but other than that, it doesn't do anything for rapid reaction or for creating a sense of urgency. Don't get me wrong, I know that we are not going to get away from the annual cycle! But you should consider installing parallel internal clocks.

The 100-day budget is a more sensible way to factor in new ideas and new projects and is a more manageable period of time. Imagine that you are rich three times a year instead of just once! People would not be delaying decisions until the next strategic review in the summer (to be followed, if you are lucky, by your plans going to the strategic approval in the autumn and then again to final approval in December, so that you can spend again in January).

Let me warn you again that reading many of these things may produce a pavlovian reaction of the type: *"Of course we won't do that! If there is an urgent need to fund something, we'll find the money."* To be fair, many very senior people think like that. But unfortunately this is not the reality for the average marketing department or R&D review meeting. The stock market calendar or measures of time that have little to do with your real needs, may have hijacked you more than you realise.

I suggest you force yourself to think about what life would look like if you were to create your own, selfish internal clocks that didn't have to follow natural calendar units or corporate reporting obligations. The 100-day budget is a good example. 100-day focus is not uncommon in politics, where we give a newcomer '100 days' to see what changes he will implement. 100 days is also artificial, but the point is that if you use it because you have decided to do so, then this is a good period for you.

Possible internal clocks that have worked well in my client work are:

- 10-day brainstorm without action, where you declare a period of continuous exploration without the need to 'start doing things' (some of your doers may start having withdrawal symptoms, but that's a risk you need to take).

- 90-day 'onboarding' period for people joining the company.
- 45 days post-merger: as a way to carve out a period of time where you can picture exactly what's happening on day 1 and what you will see in place by day 45. 45 is an artificial number that you can change.
- The above-mentioned 100-day budget.
- 20 days to explore options for X and come up with a decision and plan.

CREATE YOUR INTERNAL CYCLES INDEPENDENT FROM CORPORATE EXTERNAL REPORTING OBLIGATIONS (STOCK MARKET, SHAREHOLDERS). ACCOUNTANTS CAN ALWAYS LINK BOTH IF REALLY NECESSARY.

BE IN CHARGE OF YOUR OWN PACE, THE ONE THAT SUITS YOU.

HAVE COUNTDOWN CLOCKS ON THE WALL: 23 DAYS TO X; 13H 30' TO GO UNTIL THE PRESENTATION TO THE BOARD.

DEFINE YOUR '45-DAY PROJECT' AND YOUR '100-DAY BUDGET'.

USE LIFE-LINES, NOT DEADLINES. DON'T BE IN THE CADAVER BUSINESS. IF SOMETHING HAS BEEN ACHIEVED AND IS LIVE, IT IS NOT A DEAD-LINE.

140

Your own ideas/plans

....
....
....
....
....
....
....
....
....
....
....
....
....
....
....
....
....
....
....

Imagine...

Imagine that you can create a culture where a sense of urgency is the norm, a well-established behaviour. A culture with shorter cycles for debate, decisions, resource allocations, etc. What does that organisation look like? Establishing internal clocks totally designed for internal needs creates a sense of ownership and control, being on top of things, having the ability to react to things faster and to make decisions in shorter cycles. It also differentiates you from other organisations more used to standard (external) clocks and brands the organisation in a particular way. Imagine the benefits. And imagine which small initiatives you can take (perhaps one new, counterintuitive internal clock) that will spread virally as soon as people see the benefits of it. Observe the behaviours under new internal clocks.

In your organisation

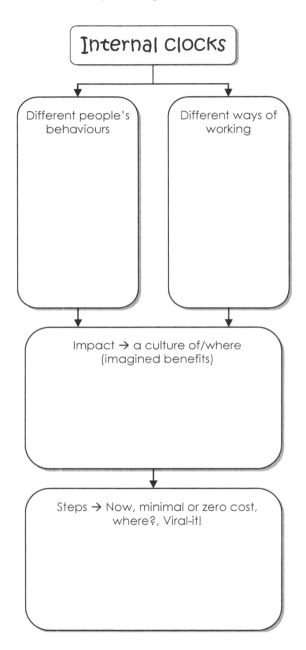

Internal Clocks

Different people's behaviours

Different ways of working

Impact → a culture of/where (imagined benefits)

Steps → Now, minimal or zero cost, where?, Viral-it!

| Processes 2 | # Decisions pushed down (and in real time) |

When a decision is made by a management team in a satisfactory way, it can create a good feeling of completion and achievement. But if that decision could have been made at a lower level in the organisation, then completion and feeling good about it don't equal effectiveness. Always push decisions down to the lowest possible level.

Decision making is a key ingredient of the operating model of any firm and it's also one that generates a lot of frustration. People want better decisions or faster ones. They complain about the lack of decisions or the difficulty making them. However, one of the key problems that I encounter in my client work is not the lack of decisions, but the abundance of them! The problem is these decisions often don't stick. Nobody really takes them seriously and people simply wait for the decision to be reversed or modified or for it to simply fade away. And *that's* the real problem!

A whole discipline of 'Decision Sciences' are taught at universities. In large organisations, some form of this may even be represented at a department or group level to assist portfolio strategy or management. But I am not talking about the mechanics or even the attributes: quality, speed, etc. I am focusing on 'where' the decisions are made. And I suggest implementing a simple disruptive rule that I call 'decision making subsidiarity'. I unashamedly borrowed the term from the European Union (EU) political jargon. In that context, subsidiarity means that if a country can do/be responsible for X, this is something country X should do/be responsible for. Or in other words: it should not be done at the higher EU level. I think this is also a key rule for organisations: if a decision can be made at a lower level, it should be made there and not higher up.

Many management committees I have worked with function very effectively, focussing on decisions made, problems solved, etc. Meetings end with a good feeling of accomplishment. I always push back: could that decision have been made somewhere else? Somewhere lower in the system? Perhaps even earlier?

If the answer is, "*Yes, our own teams could have done this actually*" or "*Yes, this could have been done at a local sales level*", then that management team is de facto hijacking decision power from somewhere else.

In the era of organisational flattening, there are less and less layers of management. We are happy about getting rid of hierarchies, but we are less good at understanding the associated liabilities. If a layer of management disappears, decision making (or 'decision rights' as it's often called) should go to the lower level and not to the higher one. A reorganisation where layers go down from 6 to 3, but where senior management absorbs most of the decision rights that became available, is a reorganisation that should raise many questions!

A consequence of decision making being pushed down is that there are many new 'decision homes' where empowered people could make a decision on the spot. One of the big problems associated with decision rights flowing upstream, to a higher level, is that these decision rights tend to go or be deferred to the management bodies that only meet from time to time! They are the antithesis of 'Team 365'.

So, pushing the decision rights down to a lower level also means that many decisions could be taken 'in real time'. Provided that people are empowered to do so, there is no reason why they should delay the decision making process. Pushing decisions downstream and making decisions 'in real time' as much as you can are two simple disruptive rules. They won't cost much but they have the power to transform your company on a big scale.

IMPLEMENT DECISION MAKING
SUBSIDIARITY ACROSS THE BOARD.

IF SOMETHING CAN BE DECIDED AT A LOWER
LEVEL, IT SHOULD. AND YOU SHOULD MAKE
IT LOWER AND LOWER ALL THE TIME.

IF NOTHING CAN BE DECIDED AT A LOWER
LEVEL, YOU ARE THE PROBLEM.

YOUR MANAGEMENT GOAL IS TO DECIDE
LESS AND LESS EVERY DAY.

'CLOSURE' AND DECISIONS MADE IN
MEETINGS AND COMMITTEES MAY BE
EFFICIENT, BUT NOT NECESSARILY
EFFECTIVE IF IT COULD HAVE BEEN DONE AT
A LOWER LEVEL.

THE AMOUNT OF 'DEFERRED DECISIONS'
(AS OPPOSED TO REAL TIME ONES) IN YOUR
ORGANISATION IS A GOOD INDICATOR OF
YOUR AGILITY AND EMPOWERMENT.

Your own ideas/plans

....
....
....
....
....
....
....
....
....
....
....
....
....
....
....
....
....
....
....
....
....

Imagine...

Imagine that decisions in your organisation are made at the right level and by the right people. Can you identify areas where decisions are very often made at a level that's either too low or too high? Many people can. Imagine that people routinely ask, "*Is this a decision that we should make/should have made*?" It creates a culture where there is a lot of clarity around accountability and where everybody is aware of each other's responsibilities and decision rights. Imagine the kind of behaviours that will be visible in the organisation. What does that culture look like? Imagine that as a result of this 'push-down', many decisions are made 'in real time'; that is, without deferring to formal meetings unless really needed. Imagine what a 'real time' culture of decisions will look like. How can you move in that direction? Can you start in some areas of the organisation and spread it virally from there?

In your organisation

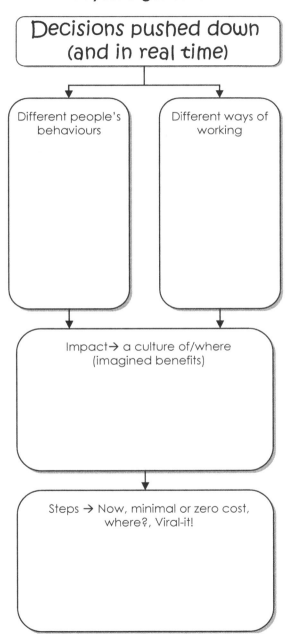

150

<table>
<tr><td>Processes 3</td><td></td></tr>
</table>

| Processes 3 | # Scan for talent, find a job |

Scanning for talent and then bringing it into the company should be part of everybody's job description, particularly at senior level. And it should be a *real* objective with consequences for their bonus, not just a nice idea they pay lip service to.

This disruptive idea is based on the subtitle of my recent book *New Leaders Wanted: Now Hiring!* (meetingminds, 2007), which is: *12 kinds of people you must find, seduce, hire and create a job for*. By suggesting this, I want to invite you to disrupt the default cycle for filling positions, i.e. have a job opening + have a headcount available → search for people → offer them a job → fill position. Instead, you should unashamedly and relentlessly scan the world for the kind of unique people you want around and create a new cycle: find the people you want → convince and *seduce* them → find a headcount. If you don't have it, romance your boss, talk someone into early retirement → hire them and then create a job for them. If you are serious about having intellectual and human capital at the core of the enterprise, there should be nothing more important to you than scanning the world for the kind of people who can make a difference and trying to get them on board. I know this is not the normal process, but then again, this is not a 'normal' book.

If you stop and think for a second, why would you want to stick with your default position and wait until you have a job opening before you start looking for the right people for your organisation? If you meet somebody completely outstanding and both of you agree that it would be an excellent idea to become partners, would you seriously consider saying: *"Sorry, but I don't have a headcount"*?

Can I also point out that you *always* have an available headcount no matter what? Because there are always people who perhaps should not be there and whose departure you have been postponing for whatever reason (unless, of course, you are in the public sector and have staff for life).

However, scanning for talent only accounts for 50% of Human Capital building; the other 50% consists of talent retention.

- ■ It should be a permanent part of everybody's job description to spot at least one key talent a year and seduce them.

- Profiling of the people-we-need (which is *not* the same as a role or job description) should be a permanent affair and a highlight of any management review (at the same level as highlighting the finances or the meeting of milestones).
- That 'role-less' profiling will force you to imagine the kind of organisation you want to build.
- The above is not just an HR responsibility. It is every manager's responsibility, period. No super-talent spotted = no bonus.

What I am saying, is that the job and role you give these people on the organisation chart is irrelevant, as long as you seduce them and hire them. Many years ago, Herb Kelleher, co-founder of Southwest Airlines, said something very important about the human capital of the company: *"we hire attitudes and then we give them the functionality we need."* And ever since then, Southwest Airlines has not ceased to be profitable.

Reversing the order of thinking in the hiring process is a contrarian idea that can pay off enormously. But it's not something everybody would be prepared to do. If you choose this from the 10+10+10=1000 menu as one of your rules, but you still want to test it out first, start with a specific department or smaller part of the company so that people can see and taste the benefits of this permanent scanning. But be bold and put it in the goals and objectives; don't just pay lip service to it. The people you can't afford not to have are out there somewhere: with your competitors, other companies or somewhere else. Make bringing them in a viral activity!

SCAN → FIND → SEDUCE → HIRE → FIND A
HEADCOUNT → FIND A JOB/ROLE.

50 % OF LEADERSHIP TIME (NOT HR
FUNCTION TIME) SHOULD BE DEDICATED TO
SCANNING FOR TALENT (AS WELL AS FOR
EMOTIONALLY AND SOCIALLY INTELLIGENT
PEOPLE).

BE OPEN TO WHAT YOU MIGHT FIND IN THE
OUTSIDE WORLD.

WHILE SCANNING, THINK ABOUT HOW
EACH PERSON COULD MAKE A DIFFERENCE
TO THE ORGANISATION, NOT ABOUT
WHETHER HE/SHE WOULD FIT ROLE
DESCRIPTION A, B, C.

PAY BIG BONUSES TO PEOPLE WHO FIND
AND HIRE EXTRAORDINARY PEOPLE AND DO
THIS AT ALL LEVELS.

156

Your own ideas/plans

....
....
....
....
....
....
....
....
....
....
....
....
....
....
....
....
....
....
....
....

Imagine...

Imagine that your organisation is permanently scanning for key talent, not as a reaction to headcount openings, not as something that happens occasionally, but as a cultural feature. Imagine that everybody has the obligation to scan for talent and bring them in and that this is included in their job description as a *real* objective, not just as a nice idea with no consequences or a bullet point on a soulless strategic plan. What kind of behaviours do you see? What kind of culture are you building? What signals is the organisation sending in terms of what matters to achieve success? Imagine that it does become a habit; something that differentiates you from your competitors; something the market will mention as: "*Here we go again: company A is hiring people again without having proper job descriptions!*" Would you feel honoured or embarrassed? Imagine the benefits of doing it anyway. Imagine the kind of conversations that you will host about the kind of company that you will constantly be (re)building.

In your organisation

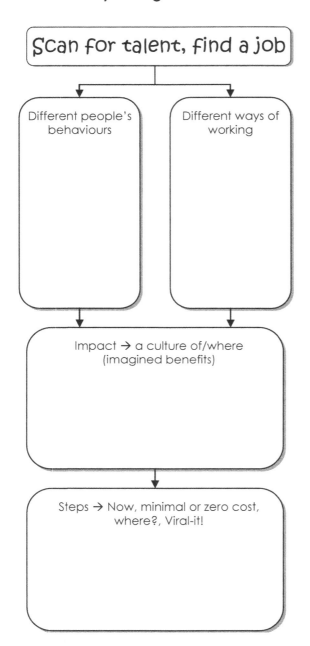

Scan for talent, find a job

Different people's behaviours

Different ways of working

Impact → a culture of/where (imagined benefits)

Steps → Now, minimal or zero cost, where?, Viral-it!

| Processes 4 | # Fix accountabilities (if nothing else) |

Accountability can not be shared, responsibility can. This simple rule will force you to rethink entire working practices.

There is a cancer in many organisations called 'lack of clarity' and which results in confusion about who is accountable for what or in charge of what. A naïve democratisation of the firm has made it politically correct to profess that everybody is 'responsible' for everything, that we all have 'collective responsibility' for things in the firm. We have mistaken this for participation, collaboration and collective intelligence. This is just one of the many things we do to make life in organisations more complicated than it should be.

I have used this rule for many years: you cannot share accountabilities, you can only share responsibilities. I thank the English language for this rule. In English, we have these two words: 'accountability' and 'responsibility'. Accountability has its roots and meaning associated with counting, take into account, called to account, account for, etc. 'Responsibility' has different roots and associated meanings: to respond, be responsive, responsible, etc.

More than one person may respond or be responsive to a problem, but only one will be called to account for the solution. There is no law that decides this! I am just taking advantage of the words' different roots in English, something I can't do in many other languages, where accountability and responsibility are the same word.

This simple rule will make you rethink entire business processes and working practices. Single point accountability is one of the most powerful rules that can be applied to processes in the organisation. Again, this is not intended to damage collective responsiveness, internal collaboration, cooperation or the desire to be more or less inclusive and gather as much intellectual capital as you can. All these are perfectly compatible with 'the buck stops here'.

These are some of the reasons why there is much confusion in organisations:

- Lack of clarity. Either people simply don't know who is accountable for what, or, very often, different people believe that they are accountable for the same thing.
- We have hammered home the idea of 'collective responsibility' and have sacrificed clarity about accountability along the way. Collegiality is great,

but only if everybody can be fired at once when a disaster occurs; otherwise it is simply an alibi for incompetence.

■ In organisations, you often hear, *"We're all in the same boat"*, but I don't know of any ship with twenty captains.

■ We rely on the existence of job/role descriptions to have an explicit reference, but they still don't guarantee that duplication of accountabilities and responsibilities will be avoided.

■ There are lots of non-accountable people whose actions (seem to) have no immediate consequence. This is a negative viral behaviour responsible for cultures where it's ok not to deliver or not to see things through.

If people in your organisation have a problem with the compatibility between 'single point accountability' (the buck stops here) and 'collective responsibility' (we are all in the same boat), then you have a deeper philosophical problem concerning clarity and transparency. The split between accountability and responsibility can bring that clarity in, can foster trust (you can trust people who don't hide behind anonymous collectivism) and can de facto create a sense of order and discipline that is usually welcomed by the majority of people.

What are the areas to fix? In a nutshell, people may be accountable for five different things:

- **Decisions**: this is one of the crucial ingredients of organisational life. Who makes the decision and who doesn't should be very clear.
- **Outcomes**: one can be accountable for a result regardless of the journey or the intervention of others needed to get there.
- **Use of resources**: allocating people and money.
- **Positions**: people should be accountable for their own judgement and position on things that matter to the organisation (strategy, implementation...) and be able to stand up for them, instead of having to use the 'they'-alibi ('they', 'the company', 'the system').
- In addition, people may decide to **take accountability** for things, particularly those that fall in no-man's land.

If you look around your organisation, you must be able to map these areas of accountability and responsibility in a way that is clear (everybody can understand it) and transparent (everybody is informed).

The reason why the title of this fourth process contains the addition 'if nothing else' is simply to stress the importance of this idea and its powerful ability to travel virally across the organisation. When people see accountability being practiced, more people will be tempted to jump in and will do the same, creating 'a culture of accountability'.

There will be many times in organisational life when not everything can be mapped, planned and predicted; when management decisions reach a good enough threshold and when, beyond that point, the implementation plan will look far from perfect. This is far more desirable than the alternative of shooting for 100% perfection and not going anywhere while you wait. In these circumstances, if you fix accountabilities and then trust the people who hold them, you've done a great job. Accountable people will then have to figure out themselves how to deal with all the gaps and ambiguities.

ACCOUNTABILITY (TO ACCOUNT) IS NOT SHARED → SINGLE POINT. RESPONSIBILITY (TO RESPOND) CAN BE SHARED.

BAN THE WORD 'THEY' (AS IN 'THEY' DON'T SUPPORT IT, 'THEY' ASKED US, 'THEY' SAID).

ASK "WHO ARE 'THEY'?" IN 90% OF THE CASES THERE IS NO 'THEY', BUT SOMETHING INVISIBLE CALLED 'THE SYSTEM' OR 'THE CULTURE' OR 'MANAGEMENT'. IT IS A PERFECT DEVICE FOR HIDING INCOMPETENCE.

BAN 'IT ISN'T MY FAULT' (OR MY DEPARTMENT'S OR MY TEAM'S).

REORGANISE, PLAN, TRANSFORM ON THE BASIS OF 'GOOD ENOUGH'.

50% HALF-DEFINED + 100% FIXED ACCOUNTABILITIES = SUPERB IMPLEMENTATION.
100% SUPERBLY DEFINED + 50% FIXED ACCOUNTABILITIES = DISASTER IN THE AIR.

Your own ideas/plans

....
....
....
....
....
....
....
....
....
....
....
....
....
....
....
....
....
....
....
....
....

Imagine...

Imagine that there is widespread clarity about who is doing what, where the buck stops in different situations, which responsibilities people share and which accountabilities are held by whom! This is a culture of clarity and transparency where duplication of efforts does not exist (or not as much). Trust will grow virally because people will see accountability in action (including both success and failure). Traditional words such as 'empowerment' and 'ownership' still have a natural home in this culture. Execution will probably be enhanced as well. Imagine that you can fix all those instances (areas, people, projects...) where accountability is not clear and that other people in managerial positions do the same. Imagine that you always act with the determination to clarify where the buck stops. Imagine that people take accountability for initiatives in grey areas, clearing up any doubt about who needs to do what.

In your organisation

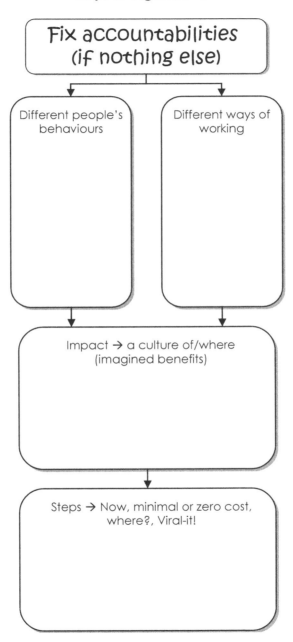

Fix accountabilities
(if nothing else)

Different people's
behaviours

Different ways of
working

Impact → a culture of/where
(imagined benefits)

Steps → Now, minimal or zero cost,
where?, Viral-it!

| Processes 5 | # Fake project, beat Outlook |

Calendars manage us and not the other way around. Protecting people's space and time is a project to be taken seriously. Treat your time and other people's time as the most important project. Apply the same discipline you use for other projects. That includes fixing meetings with yourself.

"*Time is man's last asset*", I wrote many years ago in an article and I repeated it in my book *The Leader with Seven Faces* (meetingminds, 2006) Today, life in some organisations is governed by the kind of automatic calendar (mis)management that blocks your time when you're invited to meetings. There are no gaps, no spaces and no availability. We have converted business into busy-ness. I'm sure you can identify yourself with this picture. Calendars manage us; we no longer manage our calendars. In this time famine - as it has been called for decades now by many sociologists - there is little or no available personal space to think, reflect or even plan. With no available space and time, management merely manages the inevitable: that is, things that will happen anyway. But the interesting thing is that if managing your space and time were a project, you would probably take it seriously and you would like to be on top of it.

Let me remind you of what a project is, so that you can imagine what you could do with your time:

- There will be goals (you being able to make informed judgements)
- There will be deliverables (your capacity to think and perhaps your mental health!)
- There will be time allocated in your calendar (so you would block off time).
- Your secretary or assistant would pay attention and protect your commitments, saying 'no' when things occur at the same time as 'the project'.

So why not treat your personal time in the same way?

- Go to Outlook or your calendar/project management system if you have one.
- Create a project. Call it Project M (for me) or project T (for time) or....
- Block time for meetings (with yourself).
- When you get an 'automatic' meeting invitation through Outlook that you – or your assistant - need to accept or decline, you would decline it when it clashes with project M or Project T.

- If you want to allow exceptions, they should only be the same big ones that would apply to other projects, e.g. your boss needs you at an urgent meeting.

Project M or Project T must be treated as an equal of other projects. I have called it 'fake project' in the title, because it is easy to remember. But is not fake at all, it is a very real project: the protection of you capacity to think, exercise judgement or feed your mind.

Protecting space and time is *the* survival skill of today. There is no skill more important. If you master this one, the rest will be easy. I have always been very sceptical of traditional time management measures such as the ones provided by 'time management courses'. In many cases, all they do is transform busyness-1 into busyness-2 and create a sense of order and a rational approach to activity management. Though there is nothing intrinsically wrong with this, I am talking about something more serious and fundamental: the control over your calendar (instead of the calendar - the busy-ness, the multi-tasking, the incessant presenteism - controlling you).

I know that Project M (or T for time or MMH for my mental health!) is artificial and similar to all those time management practices that I tend to dislike. But I am willing to take this route for this serious issue. We are so hopelessly dependent on our circumstances that sometimes the only way to protect time is to artificially create it!

The disruptive ideas that are compiled within the 10+10+10=1000 portfolio are not only presented for your own personal benefit. I am assuming you also care about the organisational life, i.e. you and others working together. Picture this for a second: you and your colleagues in total control of your own time and totally in charge of protecting your own space!

If you start to implement 'fake' project M, you'll see that the sky won't fall. If other people imitate you, you'll soon see an organisation with more reflective power. And I can tell you that an organisation that can think is very powerful. An organisation without room and an Outlook that is booked solid for months in advance can't do much.

BUSYNESS AND BUSINESS ARE TWO
DIFFERENT WORDS.

THE FULLNESS OF YOUR OUTLOOK
CALENDAR IS NOT A CRITERIUM OF
SUCCESS. YOU CAN EVEN ARGUE THAT IT IS
THE EXACT OPPOSITE.

START PROJECT M NOW AND ENJOY THE
PLANNED MEETINGS WITH YOURSELF.
DROP SOMETHING TO MAKE ROOM FOR
PROJECT M.

QUOTE 1 FOR YOUR OFFICE:
"ALL HUMAN EVIL COMES FROM A SINGLE
CAUSE, MAN'S INABILITY TO SIT STILL IN A
ROOM." (BLAISE PASCAL)

QUOTE 2 FOR YOUR OFFICE:
"THE CEMETERIES OF THE WORLD ARE FULL
OF INDISPENSABLE MEN."
(GENERAL CHARLES DE GAULLE)

174

Your own ideas/plans

....
....
....
....
....
....
....
....
....
....
....
....
....
....
....
....
....
....
....
....

Imagine...

Imagine that people in your organisation are 'on top of things'; not by working 24 hours a day and killing themselves, but by being able to exercise judgement, reflect on data and make informed decisions. Imagine the kind of behaviours that you will see. Imagine a culture where protecting personal space and time are the norm. Imagine that you can start this somewhere and that other people will follow until the pace of fruitless busy-ness slows down and a more reflective organisation at ease with itself emerges. Imagine how you can start this journey and imagine what will follow.

In your organisation

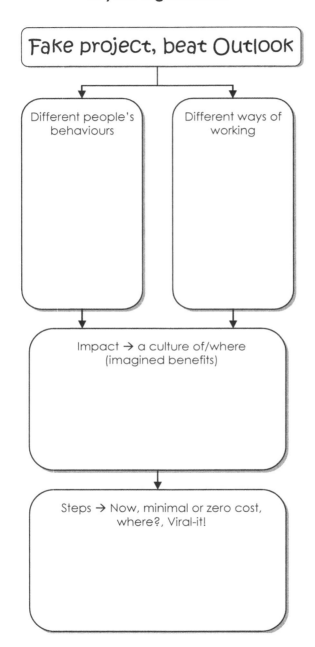

Fake project, beat Outlook

Different people's behaviours

Different ways of working

Impact → a culture of/where (imagined benefits)

Steps → Now, minimal or zero cost, where?, Viral-it!

Processes

| Processes 6 | # Un-cluttering |

Many corporate initiatives compete for airtime in the employees' hearts and minds. Unnecessary organisational complexity and its associated terminology is a significant feature of modern corporate life. You don't need re-engineering, but simple, ruthless and urgent un-cluttering. Clean up, do less.

The organisational life is cluttered. There are calendars full of activities and meetings fill the day. The internal cycles (strategic plan, business plan, next year's budget) sometimes seem to have a life of their own. People exclaim, "*I am doing the planning, the budget, the presentations... When am I going to do my actual job?*"

People also need to attend training courses, professional development programmes, maybe even a leadership initiative or a work-life balance programme. And perhaps they also need to be part of a Task Force addressing the latest not-so-good results from an Employee Satisfaction survey.

And this is just daily life; just an average random Wednesday in the life of the company. On top of all this, 'higher level' corporate frameworks do exist: there is a set of values, a set of leadership behaviours, a credo, etc. Operationally, the CEO has set the six key objectives for the year and everybody is re-drafting their goals and objectives to fit in with those. Many companies seem to be run on the basis that 90% of the focus is on managing internally/inwards and only 10% on the customer side/outwards.

All those initiatives create a corporate *'mille-feuille'* with layers that don't usually talk to each other. Sometimes their only commonality is the fact they all compete for air time. Confronted with this often overwhelming richness of corporate life, the average employee throws in the towel and switches off, unwilling to put some effort in trying to understand the connection between all the different things. In my experience with sales forces, for example, I have seen that people are given complex incentive systems and bonus schemes that come on top of the 'normal' performance appraisal. Some of those schemes seem to have been written by a quantum physicist. Management pretends that people understand the internal maths, but I have seen many good salesmen say *"whatever"*. They are no longer interested in understanding and are just trying to get on with their jobs. When I look through my client portfolio of the last five years, I could say that the average client has at least five or six major competing initiatives running 'in parallel', cluttering the airtime (not to mention an additional dozen or so minor, local or functional ones).

Un-cluttering is a truly disruptive 'anti-initiative' initiative that shouts *"Time out!"* and forces you to review what's going on and to make sense of it all. You might need to:

- postpone another initiative.
- focus on the two or three that can really make a difference. Be ruthless.
- establish a linkage between the different initiatives and develop a core values system or a true umbrella making sense of it all.

One of the key characteristics of Viral Change™, the change management approach I have pioneered, is its insistence on as much invisibility as possible. I sometimes say to clients: *"This is a cultural change management programme and this is the last time you will hear the words 'change', 'culture' or 'programme'. The best corporate initiative is the one that is silent and doesn't steal airtime."*

Un-cluttering can be done *now*. If you are in a senior management position, you could declare yourself to be the Chief Un-cluttering Officer (CUO) and you would do your organisation a big favour. It doesn't cost much and the sky won't fall down. Sure, you might upset some people with a vested interest in the cluttering, but that's a small price to pay.

This contrarian do-less *will* pay off. If this could be copied by others and if each department or group had an un-cluttering objective in their goals, the business transformation would be truly significant.

One single, common dashboard for everybody: ten parameters max; 3 'corporate initiatives' max (and that's being very generous).

Initiative/process/system test: could you explain it to your pals in the pub/bar without embarrassment?

Start an Un-cluttering Crusade in your language, acronyms and processes. End the year with less of everything and you may be more profitable!

Declare a moratorium on anything 'new': a new performance management system, a new CRM, a new work-life programme or a series of workshops. Breathe first.

Your own ideas/plans

....
....
....
....
....
....
....
....
....
....
....
....
....
....
....
....
....
....
....
....

Imagine...

Imagine that your organisation only has very few corporate initiatives and that they are all concrete, easy to understand by everybody and attractive enough to get people engaged. Imagine that you can get rid of a few layers of processes and activities that are competing for airtime (attention, energy, priorities). Imagine that simplification is a feature of the culture or at least a clear direction that everybody is committed to. Imagine a culture where people don't respond with 'whatever' when asked to join 'a new programme' of any type. Imagine the behaviours in the culture. What difference do you see? What does an un-cluttered environment look like? Can you picture the benefits?

In your organisation

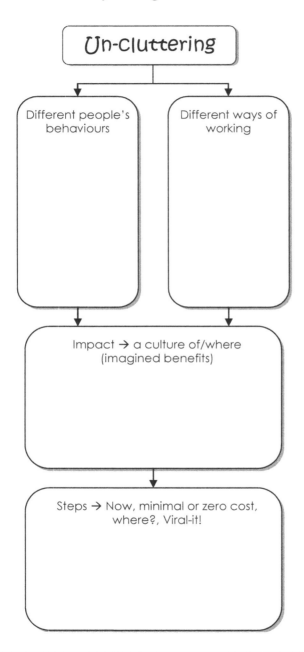

Un-Cluttering

Different people's behaviours

Different ways of working

Impact → a culture of/where (imagined benefits)

Steps → Now, minimal or zero cost, where?, Viral-it!

3-way, 365 performance appraisal

Performance appraisal should be an ongoing process, not just an end-of-year affair. It should also be 3-way: supervisor → employee; employee → supervisor and both → 'the system'. Combining this ongoing circle (top-down, bottom-up) with asking "*Do you have what you need*?" is a powerful disruptive rule leading to true transformation. I know, it's not the usual way. But it works miracles.

Many organisations have a performance appraisal system for managers and staff which has its highlights at the end of the year. At that time, a few weeks get semi-paralysed as the process of completing documents takes over. Discussions take place between managers and those managed. HR is busy reminding people of deadlines and sending guidelines to departments about how to fit their employees into the relevant Bell curve. The rhetorical dance of achievers, over-achievers, contributors, those that can do better and those with a poor performance starts. The numerical outcomes categorise the entire organisation entomologist-style: all pristine and elegant, all accompanied by a great sense of completion.

Most companies would say that the process has a strong 'personal development ethos'. In other words, it is mainly about knowing how to get better and how to develop more competencies and skills. However, there are sometimes two parallel business universes: a glorified one where the rhetoric is as above and a more prosaic one, where command and control mechanisms reign. Both may overlap.

The outcome of the performance appraisal may have implications for a salary increase or other rewards, so it is not taken lightly by people. But in managerial and behavioural terms, the end-of-year concentration on assessment, soul-searching, 'tough conversations', etc. is a very poor way of using feedback loops. In behavioural terms, the feedback, whether positive or negative, needs to happen almost instantly. Managers are supposed to 'feed back' on the spot. Recognising positive contributions is something that needs to be associated with the event, if there is one. If it's about continuous good contributions, then recognition needs to come in frequently, but not constantly and at random. Dealing with a negative performance needs to be dealt with timely as well, preferably in the form of finding alternative 'good bits of performance' to reinforce and to point in the right direction. One way or another, the end-of-year 'balance sheet' is hardly efficacious. In the absence of an alternative, an end-of-year system may be welcome, but that doesn't make it ideal.

A shift from an end-of-year to an ongoing performance appraisal brings significant benefits:

- It is likely to get rid of the ritualistic aspect of the end-of-year appraisal, where everything gets a bit paralysed and human emotions (expectations, disagreements, 'tough conversations', overdoses of praise) dominate the environment, more often than not distracting people from the business of doing business.
- Redirection of negative performance is dealt with on the spot.
- Reward and recognition are timely associated with performance, building a case for monetary reward if this is one of the possibilities.
- It would avoid the end-of-year 'halo effect'. Very often, the end-of-year appraisals are contaminated by the emotions described above. Managers either try to be too nice as a way to end the year 'on good terms', or they are too negative, having waited all year for the opportunity to vent all their frustrations. To squeeze everything into one particular narrow window of time is a recipe for unfairness.

Taking the model of ongoing performance appraisal seriously would mean that you would have frequent appraisal discussions and provide frequent re-direction/coaching. Taking it to the extreme would mean that there is no such thing as an end-of-year review because it would just be a consolidation of a continuum, i.e. the end-of-year review would be of no greater relevance than the last one held during the year. You would de facto be installing your own internal clock for dealing with performance. You are in charge and not your calendar.

Many people are stuck somewhere in between and have performance reviews twice a year. This is certainly better than one at the end of the year, but in reality it doesn't change the philosophy of a punctuated review. The true small revolution I am suggesting is that you suppress the Big Formalities in favour of a continuous effort with several points of check up, review and dialogue during the year.

As well as being a 365-affair, performance appraisals should also be 3-way, not just one way. The first one is manager appraising staff as done traditionally. It should be followed by the other way around, by the manager asking, *"Have I helped you? Can I do other things for you? How am I doing, helping you as your manager?"* This is far from a naïve, romantic or pseudo-democratic process. Managers should receive feedback at the same time as they give it. If this is the norm or if it spreads virally, the credibility and trust grow exponentially. It works wonders. The third way is both manager and staff appraising 'the system'. This means they both (i.e. both manger and staff) need to answer the question: *"Do we have/Have we had the tools to do my/our job?"* In other words, is the organisation providing the processes and systems suited to get the job done? This interrogation of the system is extremely healthy. In some (but not all) cases, managers may have to take action and provide for different support in the future. It is vital that the appraisal is done 'as a circle' consisting of these three components. In this way, 365 performance appraisals become a continuous source of improvement, trust generation and organisation building, instead of just a command-and-control, unilateral, top-down exercise.

APPRAISAL SHOULD BE 3-WAY: MANAGER → EMPLOYEE; EMPLOYEE → MANAGER AND BOTH → THE ORGANISATION AND ITS TOOLS.

IN ANY CASE:
1. BUILDING MODE VERSUS COMMAND-AND-CONTROL.
2. DIALOGUE VERSUS INTERROGATION.
3. ONGOING VERSUS END OF YEAR OR 2X YEAR.

APPRAISAL TIME IS AIRTIME, IS BEHAVIOURAL REINFORCEMENT TIME. WHAT DO YOU TALK ABOUT? 'MAKING THE NUMBERS'? DEVELOPING YOUR PEOPLE? OPENING A NEW MARKET? LEADING A TEAM?

ALLOCATION OF PERCENTAGES AND WEIGHTS IS STANDARD PRACTICE. TIP: DON'T BOTHER WITH ANYTHING BELOW 10%.

Your own ideas/plans

....
....
....
....
....
....
....
....
....
....
....
....
....
....
....
....
....
....
....
....

Imagine...

Imagine that performance appraisal truly is a continuous affair, with as many or as little review points as needed, but definitely without waiting for an end-of-year review. Imagine the different interactions and discussions between managers and staff on an ongoing basis. Imagine the risks and the benefits. What kind of behaviours are visible? Imagine a culture where feedback (of any kind) and recognition are given on the spot, as part of the daily routine, and not as a 'formal management event' once or twice a year. Imagine the kind of culture that is created when performance appraisals are a true continuous exercise. Imagine that it works and that as a result there are no more formal mid-year or end-of-year reviews. What kind of culture will that be? Imagine that the focus manager → employee is shifted to work both ways (manager and employee) and that it also looks into how the organisation provides tools, processes and systems to do the job. Imagine that the healthy questioning of how the organisation facilitates our work is a non-threatening, routine activity. Imagine the kind of behaviours that will be visible.

In your organisation

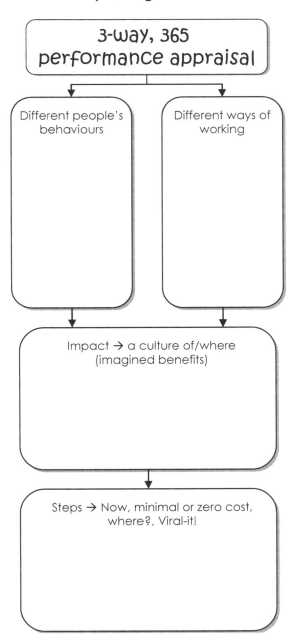

Processes 8

Face it, don't email it

Reducing email communication in favour of more direct 'face-to-face' contact is in itself a powerful way of transforming the corporate environment and of boosting precious social skills. E-mail is as addictive as slot machine gambling, but it has not been recognised as an illness yet.

Another form of organisational cluttering can be found in the company's communication 'pipes', with email having become the pervasive, used-for-everything tool. From a functional email with a long document attached which you are supposed to download, to a short 'I agree', the email is ubiquitous.

When email took over from the fax or the telephone, it was hard to believe that anything could ever take over from the email. Instant messaging didn't exist, let alone a corporate blog (where you can write/comments in real time for everybody to see) or a corporate wiki (where you can edit anything public in real time). But email is still dominating the communication channels and in some cases it has become something that sucks up a great deal of your time.

Based on my behavioural sciences background, I can tell you that there is a very good reason why email is so addictive. Email and slot machines share the same principle of 'intermittent reinforcement' which is the most powerful of all types of behavioural reinforcement our brain likes. On a slot machine, you try several times and the prize comes to you at a random and unpredictable time, so you keep trying 'just in case'. Your reward does not come after a fixed number of tries or at a fixed-time interval. That is what makes it so powerful compared to other reinforcement mechanisms where the reward comes at predictable and fixed intervals (monthly salary, annual bonuses).

In email, you leave your communication channel open and you get an enormous amount of messages. Most are rubbish, mixed with the occasional, random and unpredictable email from your boss that you need to reply to immediately or the unexpected news you have to react to on the spot. So you keep your channel open and live 'just in case', staring at the screen from time to time when your PC beeps to tells you that 'you have mail'. Blackberry is no different, just in size. The reward (of the piece-not-to-be-missed) comes at random.

There are other reasons why email has taken over. Amongst others, it is an efficient way to record everything, including the fact that you are recording... In other words, you are covering your back by electronically recording your input on an issue or a problem that needs to be solved, etc.

Emailing people sitting next to you doesn't do much to enhance your social skills either. Face-to-face, person-to-person conversations have been substituted by an email-cluttered environment, which has eroded the individual and collective emotional and social intelligence. Of course email is a fantastic tool! And it is great that we are able to use it. But it has hijacked all other forms of communication and therefore it has become a liability in many cases.

I think this is well-known to may organisations as many corporate environments have put in place some sort of measures. Those measures are usually of the restrictive-dictatorial type: limited inbox capacity controlled by IT, policy of 'no emails on Friday' or 'email shut down for a few hours', etc. They all have limited utility.

The fundamental change needed is behavioural and the above restrictive measures only have varying degrees of power to trigger or induce behaviours. Instead of restricting (penalising) email, we need to reinforce (reward) alternative options:

■ Opt for face-to-face conversations whenever possible. Only use email after you've ruled out alternative means. Can you pick up the phone? Can you see the person face-to-face?

■ Depending on the technology available in your organisation, use text messages or a blog for short communications (like your teenage daughter does) or a document management system to input/work on documents. Stop sending different versions of documents by email.

■ Make the point of enhancing communication and collaboration by having personalised interactions whenever possible. The fact that in some (many?) cases this is not possible, does not mean you should give up across the board. People are still sending emails to other people on the same floor for no particular reason.

■ ANY decrease in email traffic is revolutionary. Do not respond to emails unless you are the main recipient (So, no reply to emails for which you are only 'cc' or 'bcc'). And only respond to the inevitable ones.

I am using 'face-to-face' in a broad sense here and I'm taking the liberty of including picking up the phone. Anything that could be done in real time, using audio channels (such as telephone, webcam, Skype, etc.) or visual means (body language in face-to-face conversations or conversations via webcam), is better than clogging up the system with emails. Anything you can do to 'face it' will progressively disrupt the (cluttered) status quo and generate completely different working practices. Find out what will work for you and start somewhere soon.

DON'T START AN ANTI-EMAIL CAMPAIGN, BUT A PRO FACE-TO-FACE ONE THAT FOSTERS THE HIGHEST POSSIBLE HUMAN INTERACTION.

IF EMAIL ADDICTION IS WIDESPREAD, A BENIGN DICTATORSHIP REGIME MAY WORK:
1. DON'T EVER REPLY WHEN ONLY CC'D.
2. IF YOU NEED TO REPLY, TRY FACE-TO-FACE OR TELEPHONE FIRST.
3. DON'T USE CIRCULATION LISTS.
4. TURN OFF YOUR PC OR BLACKBERRY WHEN DONE WORKING.
5. NEVER REPLY TO OR ACKNOWLEDGE EMAILS WRITTEN BY SOMEBODY COVERING THEIR BACK.

THIS REGIME IS NO CURE FOR BAD COMMUNICATION HABITS, IT JUST EASES THE PAIN. EXPLORE ALL POSSIBLE ALTERNATIVE TOOLS SUCH AS BLOGS, WIKIS AND TEXT MESSAGE. PROTECT INTERPERSONAL, FACE-TO-FACE SOCIAL SKILLS AT ALL COST.

Your own ideas/plans

....
....
....
....
....
....
....
....
....
....
....
....
....
....
....
....
....
....
....

Imagine...

Imagine that face-to-face and direct, real-time communications are the norm in your organisation. That email has not taken over all communications and that the company is blessed with different styles of personalised information sharing and social relationships. What is different? What kind of culture do you see? Imagine the behaviours you will see. Imagine that people pick up the phone first and/or try to establish a personalised dialogue, only using email as a secondary option. Imagine what the environment will look like. What are the gains? What can you lose? Imagine a reduction of 50% or 30% or even 10% of email traffic. Imagine the change in behaviours.

In your organisation

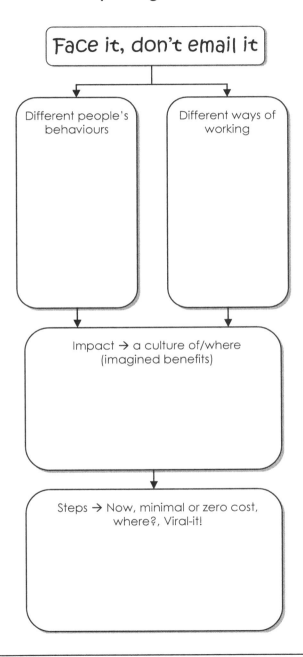

Processes 9

Less PowerPoint, more stories

Stories travel better across the organisation than clinical PowerPoint presentations. They have the power to create organisational glue. Switching to stories and slide-less presentations is a small revolution in itself, but with great positive consequences.

Stories are the natural vehicle of learning. Stories form the basis of the world's religions; they are used to pass on traditions; they are the cohesive force between people in any community from remote Polynesia to suburban London, and they provide a comfortable closure of a child's day at bedtime. Stories create literature, plays, a Hollywood script and they're even at the heart of everyone's recollection of events in old age. Stories define political and geographical boundaries. They induce laughter, fear, hope and revulsion. Stories make the news every day. Stories don't need to be defined, we all *are* a story.

In organisational life, we also have stories: heroic stories, gossip, talk about people's behaviours, market adventures... But we have completely underestimated their power and have favoured the clinical set of bullet points and PowerPoint slides. The language of bullet point lists is factual and descriptive. People remember stories more easily. They have more difficulty remembering the six strategic objectives and the ten core values presented on screen. Because you can't encapsulate a story in a bullet point list on a PowerPoint slide, stories have not been given the same status as other 'presentational' forms.

- If you want to ask people for resilience, you would be better off telling a story about somebody's resilience in dealing with a difficult customer.
- If you want to describe accountability, you would be better off telling a story about somebody taking action in a way you can only call accountable.
- If you want to tell your people that innovation is key to the organisation, you should tell a story about a group of people that systematically asked, "*Can it be done differently?*" and in doing so came up with a different solution to a recurrent problem.
- If you want to declare honesty, integrity and collaboration your three key values, you'd better have good stories about what each of these 'things' look like when practiced, because this is the best way for people to remember honesty, integrity and collaboration.

The best stories in organisational life are the ones that:

- **Engage people:** those listening can relate to them; the stories may even feel 'transferable' (*"The story is not about my department, but I can find commonalities"*).
- **Describe behaviour:** they mention what people did (or didn't do) in a way that can be modelled. (*"Aha! If this is what it is, then it is about..."*)
- **Are 'sticky':** they 'stick' to people's minds, making it easy to remember (*"I remember, it's simple enough."*)
- **Mobilise people:** to act, create 'buy in' and show more and more possibilities for everybody to explore (*"Aha, we could do the same or we could try out B or C."*)

Stories are the main organisational glue and storytelling is an art intrinsically linked to good leadership. There are lots of things that need a PowerPoint presentation, but many more that don't. Think of how you act outside your management life. How many times have you used PowerPoint to tell a friend about something? We have converted organisational life into a long 'presentation' and we have somewhat lost the ability to engage people the way stories do. But we can remedy that!

- Try giving your next presentation without slides. If you want to go even further, restrict slides to particular presentations, for example for financial data only.
- Try to seek/create stories that explain different wanted behaviours.
- Ask your people to spot and share stories about colleagues dealing with customers.
- Create a competition for good/best stories.
- Practice verbal presentations, asking people for five-minute summaries or updates.

It is something to practice and inject into the organisation and the best way to do so is by example so that it can be imitated virally. Stories have great power to transform the way we learn inside the firm! But it is very easy to revert back to your default position of using stacks of slides. At one of my presentations on storytelling I used lots of slides to explain what storytelling was! My audience laughed and pointed out how I was contradicting myself. Now that's a story I will always remember!

ORGANISATIONAL LIFE IS NOT A PRESENTATION, IT'S A CONVERSATION. SWITCH FROM PRESENTATION MODE TO CONVERSATION MODE.

IMAGINE A SUCCESS STORY THAT YOU WOULD LIKE TO HEAR ABOUT YOUR ORGANISATION. THEN IMAGINE THE SAME SUCCESS PRESENTED TO YOU IN BULLET POINTS ON A POWERPOINT SLIDE. CHOOSE!

TELL A STORY TO DESCRIBE STRATEGY, TO EXPLAIN DESIRABLE BEHAVIOURS, TO ILLUSTRATE THE KIND OF CUSTOMER INTERACTION THAT YOU WANT.

BRING AS MUCH STORYTELLING TO THE ORGANISATIONAL/BUSINESS LIFE AS YOU PROBABLE USE IN YOUR 'OTHER LIFE' AND ENJOY IT!

Your own ideas/plans

....
....
....
....
....
....
....
....
....
....
....
....
....
....
....
....
....
....
....
....

Imagine...

Imagine that there are fewer presentations and more stories in your organisation: customer stories, people stories, group stories. Imagine that your culture is one where examples of behaviours, mistakes and successes are told in story form. What does that environment look like? What kind of new behaviours do you see? What are the benefits? What do you have to lose? Imagine that you only use slides for financial data or product management. Imagine yourself giving a presentation without slides. Imagine that you ask your people to report on stories, not on Gann charts. Imagine the small organisational revolution. Imagine how the art of sharing real life achievements, mistakes, worries and hopes will grow. Imagine where you will start.

In your organisation

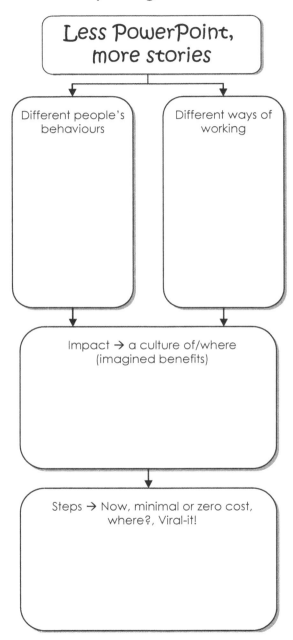

Less PowerPoint, more stories

Different people's behaviours

Different ways of working

Impact → a culture of/where (imagined benefits)

Steps → Now, minimal or zero cost, where?, Viral-it!

Processes 10

Be imperfect

Risk and reward are related. The perfect, risk-free way of doing things has no room in today's organisation. A fast moving enterprise requires a constant 'prototyping' philosophy based on imperfection. Keep your company in 'beta-test mode' as much as you can.

One of the greatest signs of maturity in an organisation is its ability to function well in 'good enough' mode. Every time I have dealt with business people striving for perfection, I have found an organisation lacking in self-confidence, unable to function well without controlling a lot of risk. As a result, perfect things are achieved, but they are also late and not terribly innovative. You will argue that many manufacturing processes and/or regulated product development can not possibly function in 'good enough' mode. I agree, but we have extended the famous slogan 'Doing it right the first time' to all aspects of organisational life. For many things, 'doing it right the first time' doesn't make a lot of sense because they require a real process of trial and error to find an acceptable outcome. There is a whole philosophical and practical management movement (with Japanese roots) that sees trying and prototyping as the real thing. Here, imperfection is the norm and the only way to get closer to perfection faster.

Organisations that function in 'perfect mode' - even if they don't accept this terminology - are those where you can see people:

- who need to have all the data/facts all the time.
- systematically exploring all the options to the point where all time is spent in exploration.
- waiting for the next set of data before moving on to the next level of decision making.
- only opting for solutions with a more than 80% probability of success.
- afraid of making mistakes.
- using a disproportionate rhetoric about quality

Unfortunately, real life is not about having all the facts and all the data or about functioning in a risk-free environment.

Somebody once said, "*no risk = no profit*". Being imperfect by design means you accept that there are levels of risk (i.e. not knowing all the data) and that you need to assess the trade-off between those risks and speed or the need to rule out unworkable options as fast as possible. When there are many choices, 'failing faster' is in a strategy in itself. Choosing an option that's 80% good will keep you moving. Choosing one that's 100% good will require you to slow down and re-analyse things all the time.

Imperfection by design means that there is going to be more ventilation of mistakes and that that's necessary. Mistake management is one of those ideas many organisations just pay lip service to. *"Learn from your mistakes"*, management says, but what they very often mean is, *"Learn from previous mistakes and if you make new ones, be careful about where you make them and how big they are."* The philosophy of truly learning from your mistakes needs social validation inside the firm. That is, you need to show that people who made mistakes are promoted in their career and can reach higher levels. Many executive boardrooms are filled with people who never made a mistake. Many of those people are not memorable or can't point to any personal breakthrough achievement other than reaching higher levels of management.

To accept and embrace imperfection and mistakes as a path to progress means that there will be practical and visible implications:

■ Create the Hall of Fame of Mistakes where mistakes are publicly displayed. Once you start (and if you are in senior management, I suggest you put your mistakes up first), it will be contagious and people will have no problem sharing them.

- Ask for decisions based on imperfect data and the associated risk assessment.
- Accept lower probabilities of success.
- Spend time on scenario planning and discussion, on exploring and 'prototyping' ideas.
- Have conversations about risks and their behavioural consequences.
- Police, spot and highlight instances where mistakes have been punished.

Being imperfect and accepting that 80% of 'completion' is perhaps good enough to move forward is a potentially revolutionary idea which could transform the business! Before you dismiss it as something that you are already doing, be sincere and see how open you really are about sharing mistakes.

Practice 'good enough' and 'higher risk'. It is therapeutic, though painful at first.

Keep 'doing it right the first time' for life-saving hospital operations.

Keep many parts of the company 'in beta-test mode', improving continuously, but never reaching a 'final', 'stable' and 'consolidated' state.

A permanent state of becoming is stronger than 'destination reached'.

Create The Hall of Fame of Mistakes and keep adding to it until it becomes second nature.

218

Your own ideas/plans

....

....

....

....

....

....

....

....

....

....

....

....

....

....

....

....

....

....

....

....

Imagine...

Imagine that there is great openness about and real acceptance of mistakes in your organisation. Imagine a culture where achievements are celebrated at the same level as the mistakes that changed the course of events. Imagine that senior people are open about what they have learnt from taking a few wrong turns on the road to success. What kind of behaviours do you see? Imagine a culture where ideas are tested and prototyped without the need for a full business plan. Imagine that your levels of acceptable risk are higher. Can you picture the pros and cons? Imagine the behaviours in a culture where people make decisions with a clear risk assessment and where there is a transparent awareness of the balance between risk control and moving forward. Imagine what will happen to the fear of mistakes, openness, credibility, etc.

In your organisation

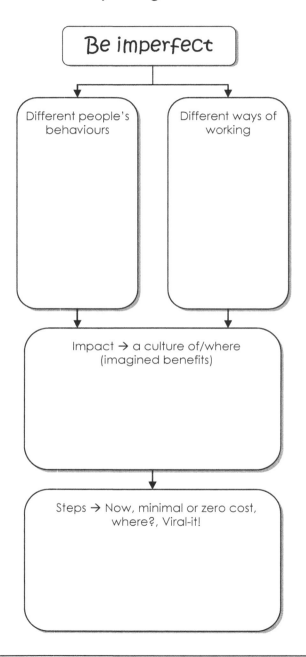

Be imperfect

Different people's behaviours

Different ways of working

Impact → a culture of/where (imagined benefits)

Steps → Now, minimal or zero cost, where?, Viral-it!

Behaviours

1 Go to source (and turn the volume down)
2 Keep promises
3 Collaboration ('the volunteers')
4 Reward outputs
5 Behave like an investor
6 Respect the past, leave it to archaeologists
7 Ask *the* question
8 Lose control
9 Can it be done differently?
10 Talk the walk

Behaviours 1	Go to source (and turn the volume down)

Invalidated rumours (corporate, project, group, individuals), minor issues and personal or group fears are reinforced by passing them along. There is only a fine line between benign rumours and a toxic atmosphere. Also, half-truths have a tendency to spread faster than the real truth. By constantly decreasing the decibels and going to the primary source of information to clarify issues, you will detox the organisation fast and you will create a culture of transparency.

In any organisation you have 'hi-fiers' and 'buffers'. 'Hi-fiers' are people who enjoy amplifying things (challenges, uncertainties, fears) and who have mastered the skill of 'decibel boosting'. They increase the organisational noise with statements such as *"We have a huge communication problem!"* or *"This is the most complex organisation ever!"* 'Buffers' are people who tend to calm things down and effectively lower the volume. Whilst 'buffers' may on occasion be 'Houston-we-have-a-problem' people, 'hi-fiers' are always 'world-we-have-a-problem-the-sky-is-falling' people. One of the best ways to turn the volume down is to go to source and bypass all the amplifier nodes!

The 'go to source' behaviour has enormous potential to transform the organisation's internal communication fabric. Organisations often create a cloud of gossip, assumptions and second-hand information that floats around, preventing sunshine from getting through. Some of it is inevitable, because it is the natural by-product of human interaction. There will always be things that were misinterpreted or half-baked information that was passed on in several directions.

The issue is not about how you suppress all this, but about how you can create mechanisms to compensate for this side-effect. Distance (remote teams in transatlantic sites, HQ - field reps, etc.) doesn't help, but it is not the main cause of the problem. Inside an organisation, Chinese whispers can be very dangerous. Some examples:

- The project is going to be discontinued.
- We are going to be acquired.
- Somebody in sales said we don't need document A anymore.
- The CEO is not happy.
- The CEO is happy.
- Somebody in X said that our data was poor.
- Somebody in Y has a complaint about us.

Behaviours

- It's going to get worse/better.
- We have a big problem.
- Employees are unsatisfied.
- Morale is low.

You'll see that the above list is a mixed bag. Some things may be theoretically easy to validate (ask the CEO if he is happy, find out from N if he really said that our data was poor), others are almost impossible to check unless you have ALL the data (employees are unsatisfied, morale is low).

However, all of them share the ability to snow-ball and become validated by the power of Chinese whispers. They are viral, but often not in a positive way!

You could preach to the organisation on this: "*don't spread rumours, wait for official announcements, don't comment on (guess about) anything unless you have 100% of the facts...*" It won't work. The measures to tackle this cloud of 'he said/she said' are behavioural and equally viral:

- **Go to the source**. If somebody tells you that 'somebody said', find the source and ask. You will see you will only need to do this a few times to decrease the number of people saying, "*I am told that he said...*" Bypass the whispers and go straight to the start. Do whatever it takes to get straight to the origin of the chain to clarify the information.

- **Decrease the noise.** As I said at the beginning, in any organisation there are people who act as *hi-fiers*: they increase the organisational decibels. Most of them are not malicious. Don't reinforce this behaviour by sending an email to the entire department asking for clarification. Even if that may be a logical thing to do, all it will do is increase the noise and thicken the cloud.

- '**Validate the statistics**'. Nine out of ten times when a client tells me, *"Group A is very disengaged"* or *"We are beginning to have problem Y"* or, simply, *"people now say that"*, I need to ask the question: *"How many people?"* Organisations have an incredible ability to extrapolate the norm from the few who express their views. I have seen the power one single individual can have in a group of fifty to unconsciously achieve the goal of convincing the Managing Director that *"We have a problem"*. (Don't dismiss this power because you feel that that particular individual is just more vocal than the rest and is simply expressing something that other people are unable or unwilling to say. You may be right, but then again, you may also be wrong.)

If 'go to source' is practiced, its viral effect will be visible in the short term: fewer people will produce invalidated and half-baked assumptions in the (mostly unconscious) hope they will get attention. The chain of Chinese whispers will definitely be shorter!

The first time you actually 'go to source', it may be unexpected or even shocking. The second time you may already be welcomed. If spread virally as a behaviour, you create a culture of transparency in which half-truths and rumours fade because they simply no longer have reason to exist.

TURN THE VOLUME DOWN! ALWAYS DECREASE ORGANISATIONAL DECIBELS EVEN IF PEOPLE ARE TALKING ABOUT A LEGITIMATE PROBLEM.

MAKE 'BYPASS HIERARCHY' A DESIRABLE BEHAVIOUR TO DEAL WITH HALF-TRUTHS AND RUMOURS. PEOPLE WILL ABUSE IT LESS THAN YOU THINK.

WHEN SPREAD VIRALLY, TRUE TRANSPARENCY WILL FOLLOW.

DON'T LET HALF-TRUTHS, RUMOURS (CORPORATE, PROJECT, DECISION, PEOPLE) BECOME TOXIC AS THEY WILL CREATE A LIFE OF THEIR OWN.

AIM AT HAVING LOTS OF 'BUFFERS' AND AS FEW 'HI-FIERS' AS POSSIBLE!

Your ideas/your plans

....

....

....

....

....

....

....

....

....

....

....

....

....

....

....

....

....

....

....

....

Imagine...

Imagine that 'go to source' is a routine behaviour in the organisation. Imagine that the chains of Chinese whispers are relatively short because people have a habit of validating half-baked information or rumours. What does the environment look like? What kind of culture are you shaping? Imagine that a few people virally spread the idea of 'decreasing the noise' at all cost, making sure that the snowball of assumptions is stopped by validating what lies behind them. What kind of behaviours do you see? What will be different? Perhaps you can start by not answering any email containing unvalidated information. Imagine a culture where blank statements such as 'we have problem X' or 'everybody is Y' are not the norm, because people take the time to assess 'numbers' in perspective. Imagine the kind of organisation and the kind of behaviours that you will see when all the above is spread virally.

In your organisation

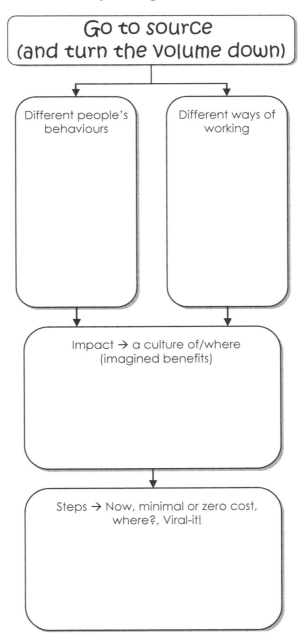

Behaviours 2

Keep promises

Keeping promises is a simple behaviour that has the power to boost accountability, credibility and trust, all in one. Just imagine for a second that everybody in your organisation keeps their promises! It's so simple that it's easily trivialised. But this simple and disruptive idea is also directly linked to employee retention...

There is a whole industry trying to provide data on why employees leave an organisation or on their level of happiness or frustration... Employers tend to like these surveys a lot: employee satisfaction, employee engagement, etc. A consistent feature in the list of 'reasons for leaving the company' is, *"My manager didn't keep his/her promises."* It is incredibly simple stuff. It is intuitive, (when we hear it, we immediately say, *"oh, sure!"*) but we usually do not grasp how important it is to people. The behavioural device of 'keeping promises' has the power to upset an entire organisation if this doesn't happen, if people don't keep their promises. On the positive side, it can also create a culture worth getting out of bed for on a Monday morning. We are not talking about grandiose promises of promotion or reward, but about more everyday, simple promises.

"Imagine that everybody keeps their promises". This is what I often ask clients to do to guide their imagination into finding out what kind of organisation they would (like to) have.

This is what the powerful and simple behaviour of 'keeping promises' does:

- It increases credibility and not just your own. It also increases the 'collective credibility' when more people do keep their promises or when it has virally become the norm.
- This is accountability in action. A 'culture of accountability' isn't created by people simply preaching the merits of being accountable, but by having people behave in certain ways.
- It creates a habit of reliability and therefore a platform for excellent execution.
- It is transferable from the inside to the outside. If your internal habit is to keep promises, why would you behave differently towards your customers?
- It forces you to go deeper into what it takes to keep your promises. Many times the attitude is good (often one of servility!), but the offer may be unrealistic compared to what can be delivered. When 'the promise' fails, all credibility goes out the

window, even if the failure was 'for a good reason'.

- It will force you to understand other people's priorities and it will put you in the shoes of people you depend on for delivering a promise somewhere else. Keeping a promise to a customer forces you to understand the constraints of the department responsible for the delivery.

- When promises are routinely kept, the organisation increases its collective trust capital.

- Keeping promises creates a 'safe' culture of interdependence that encourages interpersonal relationships, collaboration and cooperation.

'Keeping promises' as a behaviour needs to be reinforced by acknowledging it when it happens and by showing the benefits. The concept is so simple that you run the risk of it being trivialised and not taken seriously. It is worth remembering our original definition of 'disruptive idea': they are simple, cheap, can be implemented now and have enormous power if spread virally across the organisation. In my experience, this simple behaviour very quickly grabs people's attention and ranks very high in their mind. Its language is easy and noticeable (*"Here it is, I kept my promise."*) and the organisation feels the positive outcome very quickly. To introduce it you should follow the viral change principle of modelling it yourself and then letting others copy it once you have shown 'how it works'.

IF YOU WANT A CULTURE OF ACCOUNTABILITY, TRUST, CREDIBILITY, CONFIDENCE, EMPOWERMENT, RELIABILITY AND EXCELLENT EXECUTION YOU MUST INSTALL, PRACTICE AND REINFORCE ONE SINGLE BEHAVIOUR: 'WE KEEP PROMISES HERE'.

IF YOU WANT PEOPLE TO STAY IN THE ORGANISATION, DITTO.

CHANCES ARE YOUR PROMISE IS DEPENDENT ON SOMEBODY ELSE'S PROMISE TO YOU. MAKE SURE YOU WILL BE ABLE TO KEEP YOURS!

SOME PEOPLE HAVE NEVER HAD A PROBLEM WITH NOT KEEPING PROMISES BECAUSE THEY HAVE NEVER COMMITTED TO ANYTHING.

Behaviours

Your ideas/your plans

....
....
....
....
....
....
....
....
....
....
....
....
....
....
....
....
....
....
....
....

Imagine...

Imagine that people in your organisation keep their promises. Imagine that by doing so, people learn how to put themselves in other people's shoes: the shoes of those who depend on them for that promise or the ones they depend on for delivering a promise somewhere else. What kind of culture will that be? Imagine what it will do for accountability, for example. Above all, imagine the difference between rationally preaching the merits of accountability to everybody and injecting a widespread behaviour of 'keeping your promises'. Imagine what other behaviours will be linked to it. What will people do differently: what will you not see?

In your organisation

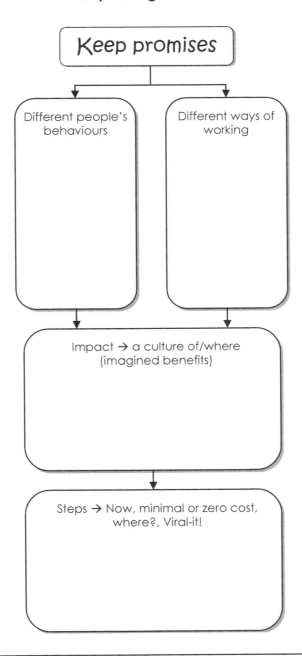

Keep promises

Different people's behaviours

Different ways of working

Impact → a culture of/where (imagined benefits)

Steps → Now, minimal or zero cost, where?, Viral-it!

Behaviours 3

Collaboration
('the volunteers')

Virtually all roles and jobs in the organisation are interdependent. Collaboration is what binds them together for success. But there is a difference between organised collaboration and collaboration as a free-floating attitude. This disruptive idea is about making everybody 'a volunteer'.

Collaboration is the new competitive advantage. The current business environment (be that in a private or public company, or an NGO) can be described with one single word: interdependence. Virtually no job can be done in isolation. Success, any kind of it, depends on somebody else's success. This is the reality, both at macro social and micro social levels.

You may think that this is just another obvious thing. After all, you have had teams and task forces for a long time and your product development or sales department can't function without the collaboration between individuals. This is true, but I am talking about a different dimension of collaboration: one that has not been designed and is not dictated (like the collaboration intrinsic to a team activity), but one that would exist even without a formal team to join. This is spontaneous, voluntary collaboration, spread across the firm well beyond teams and formal structures. These are some of its characteristics:

- Collaboration as an attitude. People are going the extra mile without the dictation of the project or the action plan.
- Embedded feeling of 'my success is your success.' It may not be an immediate quid pro quo, but we are all so interdependent that building your own success means that inevitably you're going to make sure that Mary and John also succeed.
- Making yourself available to others. In practical terms: truly *having* an open door, instead of just saying you do.

Today, a thriving culture is one where spontaneous collaboration is the norm, where 'voluntarism'[1] and 'volunteerism'[2] are present and where the opposite (individualism, silos) is unthinkable. It is a culture where informal networks constitute a truly recognisable organisational fabric. In the extreme case, everybody can talk to everybody and tap into intellectual capital wherever it is. 'Competing on collaboration' is what truly

---

[1] Voluntarism = the use of or reliance on voluntary action to carry out a policy or achieve an end.
[2] Volunteerism = the willingness of people to work on behalf of others without the expectation of pay or other tangible gain.

differentiates the thriving company from others. It is 'Collaboration-R-us'.

This attitude, if you can make it widespread, creates a distinctive culture that goes well beyond the existence of cross-functional teams, for example. We often design structures and then assume that the behaviours to sustain them will automatically follow. Creating multiple cross-functional or interdisciplinary teams is a good vehicle for collaborative work, but it doesn't guarantee that collaboration of the 'voluntary type' will be a key, fundamental behaviour. Some of the features of the collaborative culture are:

- Collaboration happens without the need to have collaborative software tools installed across the board. If the software is installed, it should build upon the existing collaborative behaviour and boost it.
- People don't talk a lot about collaboration, it just happens. The best collaborative environments I know don't spend too much time talking about collaborating.
- Information flows very freely, it is not kept in people's heads or contained within groups.
- People make an effort to understand who should (need to) know what. It is not about using distribution lists including everybody on earth, but about finding out who needs to know or be involved. It requires an active search for the kind of

information that is often not contained in the organisation charts.

- People frequently use informal channels of communication.

- People choose telephone or face-to-face communication over email.

- Joint efforts between departments 'appear' without having been designed.

- 'Membership' of informal groups is fluid.

- People's behaviours, situations and interactions pass the volunteer test. Is this something that could only happen if it were dictated or designed? Has any command-and-control mechanism been used to make this collaboration visible? Were they 'forced' to do it? If the answer is no and if it's widespread, your collaborative culture is in good shape with collaboration as a core behaviour.

I am not suggesting that all collaboration has to be of the voluntary type. There is nothing wrong with designing structures (like teams and communities) for collaboration, but this disruptive idea is not about them. It is about the collaboration that is not 'controlled', but 'volunteered'.

A few years ago, somebody working at a big, global and successful software company pointed out to me that there were about sixty or so VPs who had made so much money since the start-up, that their presence in the company was now truly 'voluntary'. They were multi-millionaires and no longer needed to be there at 08.00am every day, but they were. This is a perfect, aspirational model for today's organisations. Imagine what a company of volunteers will look like!

Boosting collaboration as a non-designed behaviour and spreading it virally is one of the best investments you can make. As with any behaviour, this spontaneous and informal behaviour that passed the volunteer test needs to be reinforced by providing airtime to it and by showcasing it. It is highly viral. Decide where to start and you'll soon see a new critical mass of people practicing it... providing you reward it every time.

AIM AT CONSTANTLY INCREASING THE NUMBER OF 'VOLUNTEERS' IN YOUR ORGANISATION.

AIM AT BECOMING 'A COMPANY OF VOLUNTEERS'.

'IT'S COLLABORATION (NOT COMPETITION), STUPID!'

YOUR MISSION STATEMENT: 'COLLABORATION-R-US'.

COLLABORATION VIA TEAMS, COMMITTEES AND TASK-FORCES IS A PASS, A BASELINE. VOLUNTARY COLLABORATION BEYOND THE DESIGNED VEHICLES IS YOUR AIM.

Your ideas/your plans

....

....

....

....

....

....

....

....

....

....

....

....

....

....

....

....

....

....

....

....

Imagine...

Imagine for a second that collaboration in your organisation is truly 'voluntary', that the culture contains a widespread attitude of helping others, seeing work as a joint effort and seeing success as the fruit of that joint effort. Imagine that many activities pass the volunteer test. What kind of organisation will you have? What kind of things will you see happening (or not happening)? Imagine that people agree that teams and committees are good structures for cooperation, but that they don't stop there. Imagine that there is a constant fluid communication across groups and teams, across departments and geographies. Imagine a company ethos where you can comfortably say that 80% of the collaborative efforts don't have a formal structure? What will working there look like? What will be the benefits? And if this all sounds attractive to you, how can you get there?

In your organisation

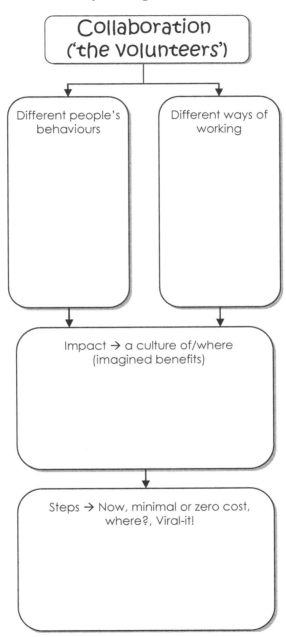

Behaviours 4

Reward outputs

In managerial terms, you reward inputs (e.g. effort) because you want outputs (e.g. productivity). In behavioural terms, if you reward inputs, you will get more inputs and not the outputs you were really after. Rewarding effort does not necessarily lead to a better outcome. It only leads to people making more efforts. And doing it systematically creates a culture where effort and not the desired result is the endpoint...

A key thing to remember is that behaviours compete for airtime. A behaviour that is rewarded or reinforced has an increased probability of sticking around. A behaviour that's not rewarded/reinforced will fade away. This is the 'abc' of behavioural management. The basics. That means that every 'activity' in the organisation, has many behaviours linked to it. For example, a high quality visit to a customer requires intellectual preparation, effort, planning time and the visit itself, which means the physical contact and the quality of the dialogue. This is very simplistic, but I am only using it as an example.

Following the simple rule of 'what you reinforce is what you get', you need to choose which competing (for airtime) aspects of 'seeing the customer' you want to see more of.

Imagine that you have 100 units of airtime/reinforcement and you use 90 of them for planning, five for the actual visit to the customer and five for intellectual preparation. If this is all you do and if you repeat it as a pattern, you would get more and more planning, but not necessarily the increase in (quality) visits to the customer you were after.

See this as an input-output model. We reward inputs (effort, preparation, planning) because, among other things, we believe in the connection input-output. But the laws of behavioural management are blind as to whether there is a connection or not. All they know is that if you reinforce Behaviour A - from a possible set of A, B and C - you'll get more A. So, in behavioural terms, if you reinforce inputs, you'll get more inputs, not more outputs. If you reinforce (reward, gratify, pay money for) the efforts that were made to achieve something, people will make more efforts, but this is no guarantee for successful results (for example, they may be the wrong efforts).

This way of 'rewarding people for their contributions' has nothing to with rewarding them for staying late at night, working weekends or long hours. If you reward the latter, those rewarded will stay even longer hours, but the question is whether their output will be better. It would be crazy to completely ignore efforts and preparations (inputs), but they should not compete in airtime (reward, recognition, reinforcement) with outputs, whatever they are: the quality of visits to the customer, the production of a report, the collaboration with colleagues.

It is extremely important to exercise continuous discipline in differentiating between inputs and outputs because that distinction between them gets blurred very easily. It is also easier to manage inputs, because they tend to be more visible: longer hours, number of meetings attended, numbers of dossiers studied, etc. However, outputs are what deliver the value to the business. If examining lots of dossiers and market research data is an output and an end, value producer in itself, then by all means reinforce it. But if studying dossiers is directed towards a better outcome (the production of a more detailed business plan or a new brand strategy), then the output is what you need to reinforce.

One extra bit of confusion: output is not necessarily the final outcome of an activity/action or the execution of a strategy. In the example used before, if you define the real output as the customer buying the product from you, then this may not even be remotely linked to the process that you are managing or that you are involved with. You need to choose or define what your outputs are. If you are in charge of market research, then the internal delivery of a report may be your output. If you are a sales manager, examining the market research data is your input, but your output is probably to create some sort of customer engagement. However, you can apply the 'reward output' philosophy in every single case.

Behavioural scientists have a word for applying reinforcements to smaller elements of the behavioural change process: shaping. It means not waiting for a final outcome, but shaping the small elements in the chain. In that context, there may be a series of inputs and outputs that together constitute the overall 'planning and preparation → outcome'. The principles still apply.

Praising efforts (input) is OK, but only if it doesn't take over and receives all the reward-capital that the output should get. This simple behavioural rule in itself has an enormous revolutionary potential. When in doubt, picture it in your head!

BEHAVIOURAL MANAGEMENT PARADOX:

IN MANAGEMENT TERMS, YOU REWARD INPUT (EFFORT, PREPARATION, TRAINING) BECAUSE YOU WANT TO CREATE OUTPUTS (PERFORMANCE, SALES, A REPORT).

IN BEHAVIOURAL TERMS, IF YOU REWARD INPUTS, YOU'LL GET MORE INPUTS, NOT OUTPUTS. TRANSLATION: REWARDING PEOPLE FOR WORKING LONG HOURS INCREASES THE NUMBER OF PEOPLE WHO WORK LONG HOURS. PERIOD.

DON'T REWARD EFFORTS IN ISOLATION. REWARD OUTPUTS/OUTCOMES FIRST, EFFORTS ('SHOWING COMMITMENT') SECOND. BUT BE AWARE: IF YOU REWARD INPUT AND OUTPUT 50-50 ("WELL, IT'S BOTH, ISN'T IT?"), YOU ARE LIKELY TO REWARD NOTHING.

256

Your own ideas/plans

....
....
....
....
....
....
....
....
....
....
....
....
....
....
....
....
....
....
....
....

Imagine...

Imagine that the culture of your organisation is very focused on outcomes. Not just on paying lip service to being focused on those outcomes ('results-focused people', 'customer-centric'), but really focused on practicing the 'reward outputs' behaviour as a norm. Imagine what people will be doing and what they will perhaps stop doing. What kind of organisation will be shaped? Imagine that you progressively focus more on outputs or outcomes and less on efforts, including the heroic ones. How can you manage that transition without de-motivating people who are genuinely supportive? A common complaint is often that people don't have anybody talk to them about their progress. Imagine that you do that, but with your eyes focused on the outputs and not on the effort or time put into it. What cultural shift will you be creating? Can you see the benefits? The challenges?

In your organisation

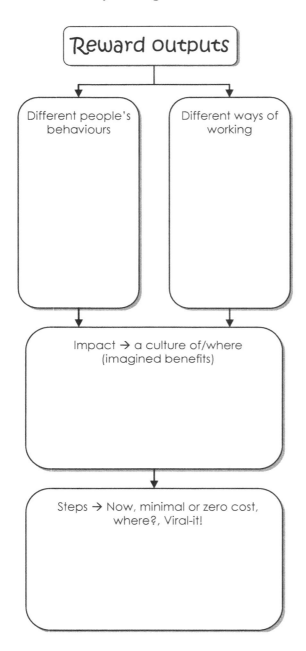

Reward outputs

Different people's behaviours

Different ways of working

Impact → a culture of/where (imagined benefits)

Steps → Now, minimal or zero cost, where?, Viral-it!

| Behaviours 5 |

Behave like an investor

Employees are investors of their own human capital. They are no different from any other kind of investor. Therefore, performance appraisals should first focus on how the (human) capital has grown. By doing this, you can transform the organisation. Everything from plain management to HR management would be completely different. Which is as scary as it is exciting.

Employees are investors. This is a crucial idea that changes everything. (It's not new, though. Tom Davenport already used it in 1999.) Employees invest their own human capital when working for an organisation. This is their asset: the combination of skills and knowledge and how they can be applied to specific roles. As investors they are paid not for the time spent in the company or for the efforts made, but for the loan and use of their (intellectual) capital to achieve specific company goals.

Also, like any investor, employees should do the math from time to time: is my capital growing? By how much? Since when? No investor will stay with a fund were there is no growth or, even worse, negative growth.

This apparently 'selfish' approach is of great benefit, not just to the employee, but to the entire organisation. Imagine an organisation where everybody behaves like an investor and is able to say at the end of each year that their investment has grown. The investors themselves would be delighted, but the fund managers (the company) would be even more so.

Behaving like an investor turns the company into a employee-centric one, which at first seems to be at odds with the well-established customer-centric one. But only the organisation that is able to grow their human capital will be useful to the customer and the shareholders in the medium and long term. The problem of who comes first in the 'Organisational Trinity' (shareholders, customers or employees) is often solved in an artificial way. People often say that shareholders come first, but also agree that nothing can happen without satisfying customers, which in turn can't happen without having satisfied employees. This chain of logic has always implied to me that the employees were nothing but a nuisance or a necessary evil. There are several permutations of the above logic chain and which permutation you choose, defines the kind of company you are. There are only very few examples of companies that declare that employees come first.

Behaving like an investor deals with the logic of the above chain by making it irrelevant. The 'fund managers' (the company, management) may focus on the shareholders - recipients of the fruits of 'the investment' - but they can't do anything without a strong focus on the employees (investors). Put in a different way, external investors put their money into the company so that internal investors can be found and brought in to invest a different form of capital. This internal investment delivers value in the form of products or services that are bought by customers. There is no longer an 'organisational Trinity', but a more mature and logical way of understanding the contractual agreements between all the players: external investors (or shareholders), internal investors (or employees), fund managers (management) and customers.

Behaving like an investor within the organisation means that things like 'effort' and 'busyness' become secondary. From the employee's perspective, being involved in 'interesting things', 'being busy' or even 'being recognised' shouldn't have any value per se, unless they could ask fundamental questions at the end of the year or at a review point:

- What is/has been my gain? What is my new market value? Have I gained new skills or updated old ones?
- What is different in my CV compared to last year's? Is there anything new, except for 'more experience' or 'another year'?

- Have my relationships grown? Do I know more people whose knowledge and experience I can tap into? Do I have more connections in my network?
- What have I leant? Do I have a new pool of ideas? Have I discovered new angles? Different approaches?

Although these are all variations of the same question (What's the investment like?), they are useful tests to understand whether the behaviour of 'behaving like an investor' has been efficient. As a behaviour, it will travel very well virally. Groups of people acting this way can easily show the fruits of their investment.

Performance appraisal systems should be completely adapted to accommodate these investment questions. If an internal investor (employee) ranks very well in 'objectives accomplished' at the end of the year, but has achieved no growth for his own human capital (i.e. the job is well done, but the employee sees no obvious gain in skills or learning, other than the time spent and the experience), then I want to point out that the overall appraisal should be negative. But it should be a double negative: for the investor (employee) *and* for the fund manager (manager). Why for the fund manager as well? Well, the latter is misusing the capital for short-term gains (achieving the annual objectives), but without adding to it (providing learning), the human capital's reuse will progressively become more limited.

As you can see, behaving like an investor - which de facto creates an employee-centric organisation - is a powerful rule/idea/behaviour. Its importance doesn't stem from any sort of pseudo-altruistic or paternalistic view about employees, but from pure market dynamics.

TRANSFORM THE ORGANISATION INTO AN INVESTMENT FUND WHERE HUMAN CAPITAL IS *THE* CAPITAL.

ONLY SELFISH 'HUMAN CAPITAL OWNERS' (EMPLOYEES) DELIVER VALUE TO THE COMPANY. NO SELFISHNESS ('MUST GROW MY HUMAN CAPITAL'), NO COMPANY GROWTH.

'EMPLOYEE AS INVESTOR' IS EMPLOYEE REVOLUTION.

THIS IS NOT PAYING LIP SERVICE TO THE IDEA OF 'PEOPLE ARE OUR MOST IMPORTANT ASSET (THE ASSET IS NOT YOURS ANYWAY). IT IS PURE INVESTMENT FUND MANAGEMENT', NO FIGURE OF SPEECH, NO METAPHOR.

Your ideas/your plans

....

....

....

....

....

....

....

....

....

....

....

....

....

....

....

....

....

....

....

....

Imagine...

Imagine that the performance appraisal system in your organisation is based on 'capital gains' and market value returns for the employee, listing all new ideas, new contacts, new skills, etc. Imagine that everybody behaves like an investor, making sure that at the end of a period there are gains to show that the investment has been worthwhile. What kind of culture/organisation will you be creating? What kind of behaviours will you see and which ones will fade? Will it be risky? What can go wrong? What will be the benefits? What kind of image will you project to the external world and how will your recruiting and retaining policies be changed? Imagine that a few people start to show the benefits and start to be very vocal about it. Imagine the implications for management and leadership.

In your organisation

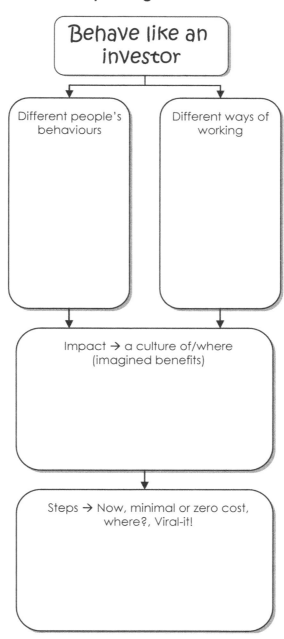

Behaviours 6

Respect the past, leave it to archaeologists

We want innovation, entrepreneurship and creativity at the speed of light ... but often still see the present as a continuation of the past. That won't work. You need to ruthlessly change focus from the past to the present and the future. If you love the past so much, you should become an archaeologist.

In today's global environment, the past may not be the best guide for dealing with the future, let alone for predicting it. Organisations, like people, face a great challenge in managing the past. How much value is there in moving forward at full speed, ignoring the past and acting as if each moment is new? And how much value is there in continuous learning from the previous experiences, the past? The latter is the more conventional teaching. But 'too much experience' is a form of baggage that stops you from approaching the future from a fresh, unbiased angle. There is a lot of value in healthy forgetfulness.

There are managers who are too attached to the past. You can identify them easily by their constant references to their previous companies or experiences: *"When I was at X..."* They can be particularly irritating at times when you want to move forward from a fresh angle. These are 10 approaches for dealing with the past:

1. **Past as pride and pillar.** Looking back, you can see the foundations, the raison d'être, the justification for today's existence.

2. **Past as baggage and shame.** Looking back, you recognise the mistakes and the liabilities; the things you wish never happened.

3. **Past as Pain.** Sometimes the past can be of a haunting nature: it is there all the time to remind you of something, to ask you for understanding/relief/an explanation.

4. **Past as vacuum filler.** People who use the past to fill a vacuum are sometimes insufficiently linked to the present.

5. **Past as comfort.** A benign form of the above, this is the 'been there, done that' approach.

6. **Past as rear-view mirror.** 'Rear-view mirror' people and organisations constantly look at the past for reference, almost automatically and unconsciously, like when driving.

7. **Past as predictor.** What happened before is seen as a good way to predict the future and therefore deal with uncertainty. People who use the past as

a predictor of the future live rather linear lives, determined by previous experiences.

8. **Past, what past?** This is another extreme, which is more frequent than you think. People and organisations can easily go into denial mode and survive like that for a long time.

9. **Past as perspective.** Some people seem to manage to use the past as a healthy perspective for their own present reality. Healthy detachment is one of the best-kept secrets.

10. **Past as a profession.** For some reason, some people choose to become historians, palaeontologists, archaeologists or psycho-analysts. They all have a (probably genetic!) fascination with the past in common.

We are what we are: it's all in our genes (genetics) and our jeans (the environment).

- Dealing with the past is an ability usually influenced by a mixture of genetic predisposition and past experiences. Organisations need to decide (and this is a good exercise) how they want to integrate the past...
- How organisations deal with their past reveals a lot about their innovative ability.
- How organisations hire people and how those people deal with the past are both good indicators of the company's values and beliefs.

You should focus uncompromisingly on the now and the future, using the past only as a reference. Most of the time organisations spend in the past is not about learning, but about 'digging'.

- Allocate a minimum amount of (protected and perhaps respectful) time to the past, but move forward quickly. Every minute spent in corporate archaeology is one less to spend on moving forward. There is only a limited amount you can learn from the past - unless you are an historian. Re-inventing and re-starting is a very healthy alternative. I am not talking about dismissing the past, but about 'using it' (and using it fast) as a way to move forward.
- Ask for historical references only as a way to frame them (i.e., how much time are we going to allocate to this?).
- Ban talk of 'when I was at X' from meetings and reviews.
- Define a time border for 'past'. Last month may be relevant, but last year or when the company was founded may not be.
- For each time that people refer to an experience from long ago, ask them to give two references for more recent ones.
- Stop using benchmarking as a safety net to know what worked in the past or what is working now. Benchmarking is a race against somebody who has already won. Find a new race. Also remember

that not all 'Best Practices' are best. In many cases, they are simply the best available, but this doesn't guarantee they are the best.

In summary: learn form the past (fast), have your feet firmly planted in the now and your eyes focused on the future.

PREFER FEED-FORWARD TO FEED-BACK. LEARN FROM THE PAST FAST SO YOU CAN SPEND MOST OF THE TIME IN FAST-FORWARD MODE.

WRITE THE SCRIPT (AND I MEAN THAT LITERALLY!) THAT EXPLAINS HOW YOU WILL GET TO THE DESIRED OUTCOME 'TOMORROW'.

BAN 'WHEN I WAS AT X' OR INVITE THOSE WHO SAY IT TO GO BACK.

NEW GAME:
INVENTING THE FUTURE: 5 – ANALYSING THE PAST: 0.

THE FUTURE IS ALREADY HAPPENING.

Your ideas/your plans

....
....
....
....
....
....
....
....
....
....
....
....
....
....
....
....
....
....
....
....

Imagine...

Imagine that the culture of the organisation is anchored healthily in the past, but with a strong focus on the present and future. Imagine an organisation where expressions such as *"When I was at X..."* are rare, not because they are wrong, but because people are applying all their energy to the present and the future. Imagine the organisation has a strong view on what its position is with regard to 'the past' (the 10 points mentioned before), but just as a way to move forward and move differently. What kind of behaviours will you see? What will be different in the daily life of teams and reviews? Imagine that the focus on the present and the future is spread virally, with only very few people in your organisation falling under the archaeologist metaphor.

In your organisation

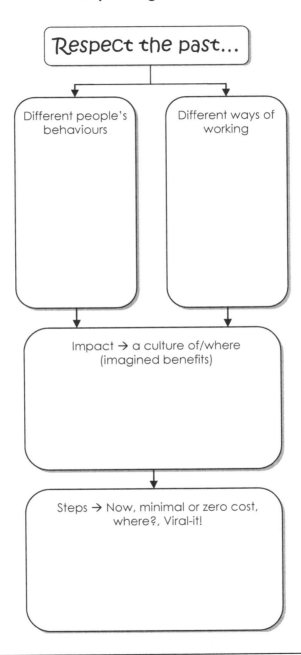

Respect the past...

Different people's behaviours

Different ways of working

Impact → a culture of/where (imagined benefits)

Steps → Now, minimal or zero cost, where?, Viral-it!

| Behaviours 7 | **Ask *the* question** |

The most fundamental and potentially disruptive management question is, "*What is the question*?" Legions of corporate troops go to work every day without having asked themselves that question... but they still provide beautiful answers nevertheless.

If we held a competition for simplicity among disruptive ideas, this one would win the prize. If you want a pure example of something disruptive (i.e., cheap, can be implemented now and has colossal disproportion between its simplicity and the impact), 'asking *the* question' would be it.

Organisations are populated by doers anxious to get into execution as soon as they see bullet points on a flipchart. There is no shortage of activities, actions, implementation points, execution of ideas, etc.

'Flawless execution' has been a mantra for many years. This has escalated to the point where we are sometimes proud of the flawless execution of a completely flawed idea. We are providing loads of beautiful answers to the wrong questions. And what's more, we are happy with those irrelevant but elegant answers! The automatic 'execution' pilot takes over without people realising that they have bypassed a small, fundamental question: "*Why are we doing this?*"

If you think this is an exaggeration, let me remind you that entire systems have been built following the internal logic and intrinsic cohesiveness of a process... and leading to major absurdities. Richard Buetow, ex-director of corporate quality at Motorola, said about a well-known quality system:

> "*With ISO 9000 you can still have terrible processes and products. You can certify a manufacturer that makes life jackets from concrete, as long as those jackets are made according to the documented procedures and the company provides next of kin with instructions on how to complain about defects.*"

The most important management question is, "*What is the question?*", and the disruptive idea is to ask it systematically! There are immediate secondary questions:

- Is the question answerable? That is, are we in position to (ever) answer it?
- What kind of answers are in our potential portfolio:

- o Technological answers: how can this be addressed from the technological viewpoint?
- o Economic answers: what are the financial answers/implications?
- o Political answers: how does it fit into the socio-political system?
- o Psychological answers: what would that mean for the behaviours of individuals?
- o Etc.

There are many potential answers and they may or may not overlap. Problems usually arise when choosing the type of answer for any question. For example, a social question may get a technological answer; a political question may get a psychological answer. These may or may not be appropriate, but you need to be conscious of the fact that your default position will only lead you to the type of answers you feel most comfortable with. I'm sure you can think of all sorts of combinations and perhaps even find examples in your organisation. So systematically asking, *"Is this kind of answer appropriate to the question?"* is an important exercise as well.

Examples of potentially disconnected questions and answers are:

- How can we create a collaborative culture? By providing collaborative software. The question is social, the answer given technical. Possible?

- How can we use a document management system more efficiently? By training people again/more. The question is technical, the answer given skill-based. Does it work?
- How can we motivate people more? By increasing salaries. The question is psychological; the answer assumes a connection with economics. Comfortable?

Asking *"What is the question?"* - i.e., what are we trying to address; what is the real issue on the table or why are we doing this? - is a behaviour that can spread virally very fast. All it takes is a few people to start the practice! The potential to re-direct ideas and avoid big fiascos is enormous.

When the 'doer community' has already marched out to the battlefield, it is too late to ask this question! And asking the question may also be irritating, because many people do not want to be questioned on issues they see as done and dusted. It may take some courage at times, but you need to remember at all times what the most important management question is, as you don't want to miss the opportunity to ask it.

THE MOST IMPORTANT QUESTIONS:

1. WHAT IS THE QUESTION? WHAT ARE WE TRYING TO ANSWER HERE?

2. WHY ARE WE DOING THIS?

3. IS THIS WHAT WE (MANAGEMENT) ARE SUPPOSED TO BE DOING?

4. GO BACK TO NUMBER ONE.

ASK THOSE QUESTIONS IN ANY REVIEW MEETING, ANY DEBATE LEADING TO DECISIONS, ANY MEETING TO DOUBLE-CHECK ON THINGS AFTER DECISIONS HAVE BEEN MADE.

284

Your ideas/your plans

....
....
....
....
....
....
....
....
....
....
....
....
....
....
....
....
....
....
....
....

Imagine...

Imagine a culture where action is not taken in automatic pilot mode, but following reflective judgement. Imagine that people routinely ask what the question behind this important project really is? What are we trying to answer? Are we looking for global, broad answers or for specific, technological ones? Are we mixing them up? What is expected? What are the real issues? Sometimes 'the questions' on the table hide another perhaps deeper and more fundamental set of questions. Imagine a culture where this kind of healthy questioning is routine and pervasive; where all the energy for execution is only applied after a vigorous challenge by 'the question', to ensure that everybody is on the same page. Imagine the kind of organisation and the kind of behaviours that you will see. Imagine the benefits of practicing this disruptive behaviour.

In your organisation

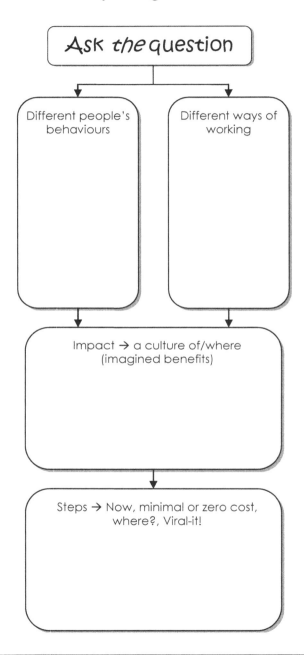

Ask *the* question

Different people's behaviours

Different ways of working

Impact → a culture of/where (imagined benefits)

Steps → Now, minimal or zero cost, where?, Viral-it!

Behaviours 8
Lose control

The more 'command-and-control' you practice, the less control you actually have and the more you'll have to command. In today's organisational life, there is little room for the 'and' between the words 'command' and 'control'. If anything, it is 'command and be a slave to it'. Lose control and you will actually gain more control.

In today's business environment, to lose control actually means having more control. If 'nuclei of control' are scattered all over the organisation and the company functions well, that is a clear sign that there is no need for a central 'command and control'. It is also an indication of distributed independence, of trust in people's capabilities spread across the organisation. Although the days when Woolworths' staff had uniforms without pockets (to make sure they didn't steal) are long gone, the days where individual employees and teams don't have much room to decide themselves (as they may make the wrong decisions) have not.

Command and control management is intellectually dismissed by many who are convinced of its inefficiency and waste. But rational understanding is not necessarily the same as emotional integration. There are many different ways in which you can exercise command and control... and you might be doing it even if you say you don't. The following are just a few examples that I frequently see in my consulting work:

- Excessive 'reporting back' points included in a project.
- Too many reviews and rehearsals of presentations.
- Pre-approval of certain types of communication outside official reporting lines.
- Decision-making powers accumulated at the top of the organisation chart.
- Devolved responsibility, but with little budgetary room for execution.
- Decision points centralised around formal meetings.

As I said, the paradox of control is that the more you let go of it, the more control you will have as there will be several 'points of control' scattered across the organisation. If you think this is something you can't afford, then that already tells you a lot about the kind of organisation you have.

The way to think about changing this is simple: what can I do to control less? What kind of changes -

perhaps structural, perhaps people-related - would I have to make in order to distribute control? If I want to lose control, I will have to trust other people in the organisation who will be sharing the control. What would prevent me from doing so? Is it the people I have? That may be part of the problem, but the problem could also be you.

Starting on this road entails first mapping the areas where control could be devolved at some risk and then taking some more risks. Here are some ideas:

- **Push down decision making.** Review decision points and delegate one to a lower level every month until you have lost most of the control. Remember, this should be the goal and you'll need to change a few things so that it is possible.

- **Allocate budgetary responsibilities** to groups or teams. In some product development organisations, budget is still very centralised so project teams are merely administrators. To push down budgetary responsibilities and 'lose some control' to the project leader, for example, could make those teams far more accountable and perhaps more business focused.

- **Suppress monthly reports.** Cascading monthly reports down the hierarchical lines is a waste. Ask everybody to post highlights of their progress online (intranet, team room, wiki, etc.) and to do so in real time. If nothing else, you will be removing an artificial internal clock.

Losing control is disruptive and powerful. It can spread virally by devolving and sharing accountabilities. But it needs to start somewhere...

HAVE A LET-GO PLAN AND ROLL IT OUT OVER WEEKS OR MONTHS. WATCH THE SKY, IT WON'T FALL.

AIM AT CONTROLLING NOTHING; THIS IS THE ONLY WAY TO BE IN CONTROL.

IN POSITIONS OF LEADERSHIP: MORE BACKSTAGE, LESS FRONT LINE.

DELEGATE UNTIL YOU GET REALLY SCARED. IF IT'S NOT SCARY, IT'S NOT RADICAL ENOUGH. TRY HARDER.

Your ideas/your plans

....
....
....
....
....
....
....
....
....
....
....
....
....
....
....
....
....
....
....
....

Imagine...

Imagine an organisation with very 'distributed' accountabilities and less centralised control. Imagine what the behaviours in that organisation look like. Imagine a culture where people are asking themselves what they could control less and where those people have a plan to decrease their levels of control, instead of one to gain more. Imagine how this can spread. Imagine what the consequences are for trust and accountability across the organisation. Imagine the kind of behaviour that will be visible. What will need to change? What are the benefits? Imagine the barriers (individual or institutional) that can appear. Imagine how you will deal with them.

In your organisation

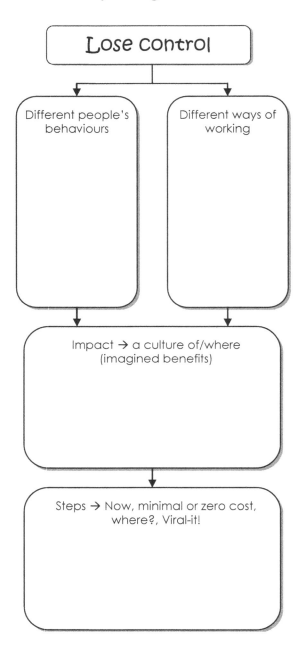

Lose control

Different people's behaviours

Different ways of working

Impact → a culture of/where (imagined benefits)

Steps → Now, minimal or zero cost, where?, Viral-it!

| Behaviours 9 | # Can it be done differently? |

There is no such thing as an innovative culture. There are only cultures where people do innovative things. 'Innovative cultures' are those created by innovative behaviours, such as seeking unpredictable answers and relentlessly asking "*Can this be done differently?*"

Innovation is hardly a new management idea. Many people think of innovation as a grandiose project with a grandiose outcome: a major breakthrough, a brand-new Apple gadget, a cure for cancer... But innovation is something that can be fostered. A culture of innovation is one where new ideas are easily generated and where 'looking for innovation' is part of the behavioural fabric of the organisation.

Reams of paper have been dedicated to innovation and I don't want to explore the theme in depth here! I am interested in disruptive ideas and there are two involving innovation. The first one is structural and I have dealt with it in the section on Structures. In a nutshell, teams are not terribly good for innovation because they tend to constitute a rather predictable environment.

My preferred way of describing how you can get innovation is 'look for unpredictable answers'. The predictable answers may refine things or solve problems, but they can hardly generate new ideas. Teams are full of predictable answers. If you work closely with John, Mary and Peter (even in a remote or virtual team, as that is still 'close'), chances are that you can 'predict' their views on things. Even if the three of them were outstanding individuals with 'lots of ideas', there would still only be three predictable sets of answers, no matter how rich they were.

Loose networks are great for innovation because you don't know the individuals well. And when you shout, *"Houston, I have a problem!"* or simply, *"Does anybody know how to get to X?",* you are literally entering uncharted territory full of possibilities.

A simple consequence of all this is that you should involve diverse people in your discussions, reviews, etc. The more people with similar ideas you have, the less innovation will come up.

A second angle of innovation is behavioural. It has to do with systematically asking *"Can this be done differently?"* Better? Cheaper? This is a discipline that can be implemented now at zero cost. Imagine that a team has just solved a crisis. Things have gone well, anxiety is down and there is satisfaction in the air. People have handled things brilliantly and efficiently. Everybody congratulates everybody. But the question is could that crisis have been solved differently? Have we solved it in the same way we solve all crises? Are we becoming proficient in solving crises? Are we perhaps creating a (scary) Crisis-Solving Best Practice here? If the answer is yes, then chances are you are not in a terribly innovative environment.

In other words, innovation as a behaviour has to do with questioning and challenging the status quo of things, seeking different angles and possibilities. Asking the question *"Can it be/could it have been done differently?"*, is a simple and disruptive yet powerful behaviour.

A necessary corollary of asking the question and feeling a bit uncomfortable with the answers is that it will force you to experiment with alternative ideas and perhaps to explore some unconventional avenues.

In my experience, the discipline of asking the question spreads very fast virally in situations such as:

- Review forums, approval bodies or committees (before the approval is granted).
- Crisis management (as above).
- Planning process.
- Post-activity reviews or 'post mortem'.

But the key to 'reinforcing innovation' is to be ruthless in deciding which behaviours to reinforce. Following the example above, if a job is well done, but it is not done in an innovative way, you should not reward it, if innovation is what you want to reward! You can't have it both ways.

EVEN IF YOU IRRITATE EVERYBODY, ASK RELENTLESSLY, "CAN IT BE DONE/COULD IT HAVE BEEN DONE DIFFERENTLY?"

ASK HOW THIS IS DONE IN X (AS FAR AWAY FROM YOU AS POSSIBLE; NOT THE TEAM NEXT DOOR OR YOUR WELL-KNOWN COMPETITOR).

IF YOU WANT INNOVATION, DON'T REWARD A JOB WELL DONE THAT DOESN'T INCLUDE INNOVATION.

IF YOU WANT TO REWARD JOBS WELL DONE, DO SO, BUT YOU WILL ALSO BE REWARDING NON-INNOVATIVE THINGS

IF YOU WANT TO REWARD BOTH, (1) YOU ARE CLOSE TO THE NORM AND (2) YOU ARE CLOSE TO NOT REWARDING ANYTHING EFFECTIVELY (TIP: CHOICE).

WATCH OUT FOR NICHOLAS NEGROPONTE'S WARNING: "INCREMENTALISM IS INNOVATION'S WORST ENEMY."

300

Your ideas/your plans

....
....
....
....
....
....
....
....
....
....
....
....
....
....
....
....
....
....
....
....

Imagine...

Imagine an organisation where looking at alternative ideas or avenues, at different ways of doing things, etc., is favoured. A culture where doing a job well isn't enough, because seeking new ways is very much present in the company's behavioural fabric. Imagine what some formal activities will look like in that culture: post-mortem reviews, 'lessons learned', crisis management... Imagine a culture where the question *"Can it be done differently?"* is spread virally across the organisation and asking it had become a habit or discipline. What will you see differently? Imagine that in this culture people will always go outside their zone of comfort to find 'the unpredictable answer'. What will people be doing differently? What will it be like to work there?

In your organisation

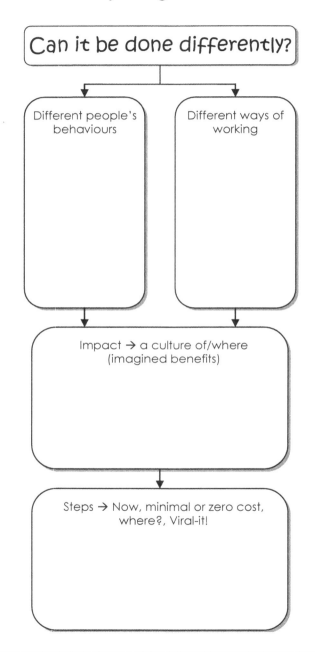

Can it be done differently?

Different people's behaviours

Different ways of working

Impact → a culture of/where (imagined benefits)

Steps → Now, minimal or zero cost, where?, Viral-it!

Talk the walk

'Walk the talk' is being consistent: say
something and then do what you said you would.
'Talk the walk' is when you act first and then follow it
up with words consistent with your actions. The former
is good management, but the latter is an extremely
powerful disruptive idea.

The expression 'walk the talk' means you do what
you ask other people to do or what you promised to do.
There are a few variations on the theme, but they all come
down to this: practice what you preach! Walking the talk is
a key behaviour in the organisation (but not a disruptive
behaviour). Walking the talk is absolutely necessary and
people who do this are true value creators in three ways:

- **They build trust**. Trust professes the most 'unfair'
  un-linearity of all: small breaches of trust have the
  power of extrapolation, generalisation and of
  triggering total defence: "*If you have failed me on
  this one, you'll do it again.*" People who walk the
  talk are reinforcing trust all the time because their

primary driver is to behave in a way that shows consistency with what they say. Some of these people do this in a rather unconscious way.

- **They are powerful role models.** The power of imitation and/or social copying is enormous. Although one could role model via language, expressions, declaration of values, etc., there is nothing more powerful than overt, observable behaviours. Most of these powerful behaviours are silent. By that I mean that they are not announced and heralded; they happen naturally, not through spin.

- **They practice behavioural translation.** Our language is full of things that we call values, beliefs, mindsets, attitudes, etc. We can have good conversations within that vocabulary, but these may happen under the false assumption that we all agree on the specific meaning of these terms. Only behaviours are observable and unequivocal. There is no such thing as honesty, at least like there is grey hair or a deep voice. There are behaviours that when exhibited we agree to call honest. From there we then infer and create 'honesty' as a value-concept. The problem with mindsets, attitudes, values, etc. is that they are not operational. We can't do much with them unless we translate those values and beliefs into observable behaviours.

All this is very well and desirable, almost a baseline. Hardly negative. You need all those behaviours and all those people big time. But the disruptive behaviour is actually the reverse of walk the talk. 'Talk the walk' goes beyond the simply necessary to find that inherent disproportion between the relatively simple behaviour and the big impact in the organisation:

- In walk the talk mode, you model the behaviour you told *other people* you want to see from them. In talk the walk, you do it first and then talk about it afterwards.
- The walk the talk wisdom would say that you should do what you say you're going to do. The talk the walk disruptive behaviour tells *you* to do it and only then to talk about what you have done and what you would like people to do as well.
- In walk the talk mode, you act following declarations. In talk the walk, you get involved personally in group activities that are strictly speaking only done by people reporting to you. You make yourself part of the team, even temporary. Walk with them and then talk about what's happening, about how people are doing.
- The talk the walk disruptive behaviour can also be described as: do more, talk less.

Talk the walk is highly viral because people will see you doing something and then they will hear about the philosophy or the rationale behind it. Seeing the behaviour is the first step to successful imitation. Start with the action, follow up with the words. It doesn't get more disruptive than that!

DO MORE, TALK LESS (AND ONLY TALK
AFTER YOU DO).

START WITH ACTION, FOLLOW WITH
EXPLANATIONS.

WALK THE TALK GENERATES TRUST.
TALK THE WALK GENERATES EXPONENTIAL
TRUST.

INVITE PEOPLE REPORTING TO YOU TO DO
THE SAME. THE VIRAL SPREAD WORKS
WONDERS.

MAKE SURE YOUR MANAGEMENT ACTIONS
ARE VISIBLE, SO THAT YOU CAN EXPLAIN
THEM TO ALL.

PEOPLE MAY GET CONFUSED ABOUT THE
LANGUAGE TRICKS (WALK THE TALK VS.
TALK THE WALK). EXPLAIN THE DIFFERENCE
AND INVITE PEOPLE TO CHANGE
BEHAVIOURS.

308

Your ideas/your plans

....
....
....
....
....
....
....
....
....
....
....
....
....
....
....
....
....
....
....
....

Imagine...

Imagine a culture with good mutual levels of trust because people do what they say they will do. Imagine a 'walk the talk' management culture where there is a clear observation of consistency between what management (or others) say they will do and what they actually do. Imagine an organisation working like that. Now imagine a culture where the action is more visible than the 'talk' and where people are going beyond the 'walk the talk' to talk about what has already been walked! Imagine the behaviours in the organisation. What will you see and what will be the benefits? Imagine what this will do for your overall trust capital. Imagine where to start building it.

In your organisation

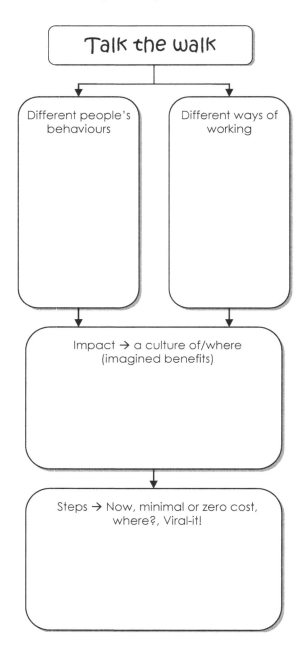

Talk the walk

Different people's behaviours

Different ways of working

Impact → a culture of/where (imagined benefits)

Steps → Now, minimal or zero cost, where?, Viral-it!

Epilogue

Where would you put your money?

Where would you put your money?

The good news is that you don't need any money. But you will have to make choices. I have offered you a 10+10+10=1000 formula, but you need to create your own mathematics.

Imagine that you have limited 'money' or a limited number of 'energy units' (a combination of effort, dedication, attention and willingness to do something about it!) and that you have to choose amongst all the disruptive ideas (for an easy overview, see the graph on page 308). What would you do? Imagine that you have 30 units. Where would you use them? It would be a terrible idea to allocate one 'energy point' to each disruptive idea, because you only need a few to have real transformation. And if you want to get serious transformation faster, do it virally. Start somewhere, choose some champions and make sure they know how to reinforce behaviours and how to spread the chosen ideas to other parts of the organisation.

The following is a suggested process for engaging your team in this line of thinking:

- Read the book.[3]
- Allocate specific ideas to specific people. Everybody reads everything, but depending on the size of your team, every person will be the sponsor of one or more specific ideas.
- Each sponsor chooses a partner to be the critic.
- When you get together, each sponsor presents (no PowerPoint!) the idea, comments on it and suggests you imagine what the organisation would look like if the idea were widespread.
- The critic then presents his views on why it may not work. Make sure that the criticism is robust, but based upon solid grounds!
- Each member of the team takes notes and at the end of each presentation privately allocates some energy points to the disruptive idea presented.[4]
- When all 30 ideas have been presented, your group members disclose their individual allocation. Depending on your environment you may want to do that on a flipchart, a board, on screen, etc.
- The debate starts. Discuss the possible significant differences between the ratings by different people!
- Reach a consensus about a few of them. Warning: there is no ideal number, but if you have more

[3] meetingminds offers discounts for bulk orders of copies. Please contact sales@meetingminds.com for more info

[4] You can download the overview graph from www.disruptiveideas.org

than ten in total, I suspect you 'want everything', which is a traditional management temptation.

- Discard anything that, for whatever reason, can't be implemented NOW. Regroup.

- At this stage you may think that you're done, but you are not. See the combination of disruptive ideas in its 10+10+10 maths. Imagine what your organisation will look like and imagine the kind of culture you will be shaping.

- Agree on a final set.

- Allocate accountabilities for implementing each disruptive idea. Remember that in viral mode you will need champions. Draw up a plan of 'where to start'.

- Off you go.

Approach the above professionally. Don't complete the whole process in less than one day. Include sufficient time for preparation and reading.

Structures   Processes   Behaviours

Structures	Processes	Behaviours
Team 365	Internal clocks	Go to source (and turn the volume down)
Double hats (one boss is not enough)	Decisions pushed down (and in real time)	Keep promises
Shadow Jobs	Scan for talent, find a job	Collaboration ('the volunteers')
Everything a project	Fix accountabilities (if nothing else)	Reward outputs
Management by invitation	Fake project, beat Outlook	Behave like an investor
Fixed-term teams	Un-cluttering	Respect the past, leave it to archaeologists
Net-work, not more teamwork	3-way, 365 performance appraisal	Ask *the* question
Support functions are businesses ('market tested')	Face it, don't email it	Lose control
Membership bids	Less PowerPoint, more stories	Can it be done differently?
Home effects	Be imperfect	Talk the walk

The disruptive ideas project

www.disruptiveideas.org

The disruptive ideas project

(www.disruptiveideas.org)

This is an evolving book and I would welcome your help in refining the ideas. I would like to learn from your experiences, so please visit **www.disruptiveideas.org** and pass on your comments for all or selected chapters/ideas.

I can't promise that all the comments will be published, but if your comments are incorporated in the mainstream page, you'll be given credit in the next edition of the book.

The possibilities to contribute are endless. For example:

- You can improve the list of examples within a disruptive idea.
- You can give examples of how something actually worked for you or how it didn't.
- You can give recommendations for the implementation of ideas.

- You can make suggestions on how you can spread the disruptive idea(s) virally.
- You can highlight a combination that has worked for you or that you think would be particularly powerful.
- You can make comments on the main text.
- You can describe the kind of organisation that would be created by applying a particular disruptive idea or several ideas.
- You can explain how you have sponsored or plan to sponsor (a) particular idea(s).

The book will be reviewed once or twice a year, so you won't have to wait years before you'll see your contributions in print! The website will tell you when the next edition is due and what the cut-off will be for that edition. One thing's for sure: every new edition will be better than the previous one!

About the author

Leandro Herrero practiced as a psychiatrist for more than fifteen years before taking up senior management positions in several leading global companies, both in Europe and the US.

He is founder and CEO of The Chalfont Project Ltd, an international consulting firm of organisational architects. Taking advantage of his behavioural sciences background – coupled with his hands-on business experience – he works with organisations of many kinds on structural and behavioural change, individual and group leadership and human collaboration.

Leandro Herrero has pioneered *Viral Change*™, a new and unconventional methodology to create fast and sustainable change in organisations.

Other than his medical and psychiatric qualifications, he holds an MBA and is Fellow of the Chartered Management Institute and the Institute of Directors (UK). He is also a member of the Advisory Board at the Operational Research Department (part of the new Department of Management) at the London School of Economics.

As a consultant, speaker and author, Leandro Herrero is at the cutting edge of modern organisational development. He has published several books, among which *The Leader with Seven Faces*, *Viral Change* and *New Leaders Wanted: Now Hiring!*

About The Chalfont Project Ltd

The Chalfont Project Ltd is an international consulting firm of organisational architects, led by the author. They work with organisations of many kinds on structural and behavioural change, organisational innovation, leadership and human collaboration.

Their website (**www.thechalfontproject.com**) offers a wealth of information on the above subjects.

If you need facilitation regarding *Disruptive Ideas* or if you would like to execute the process described in the epilogue in workshop format within your organisation, please contact ukoffice@thechalfontproject.com or call +44 (0)1494 730 999.

Viral Change:
The alternative to slow, painful and unsuccessful management of change in organisations
By Leandro Herrero

Many 'Change Management' initiatives end in fiasco, because they only focus on processes and systems. But there is no change, unless the change is behavioural.

Viral Change is THE manager's handbook on how to create sustainable and long-lasting change in organisations.

The author says: "*If change is needed, the traditional 'change management models' may not be the most effective vehicle. Most of those change management systems fail because they do not deliver behavioural change in the individuals. Viral Change is different... and it works!*"

You can listen to the author talk about *Viral Change* at **www.meetingminds.com**, where you can also read excerpts, reviews and much more.

Viral Change is available from Amazon, Barnes and Noble, Blackwell, WH Smith, Borders, Books Etc. and many other (online) bookshops, as well as from www.meetingminds.com.

The Leader with Seven Faces:
Finding your own ways of practicing leadership in today's organisation

By Leandro Herrero

After all the books written about leadership, you'd think we know a thing or two about leadership. However, nothing seems to be further from the truth.

The Leader with Seven Faces provides a novel approach to leadership where the questions to ask (about what leaders say, where they go, what they build, care about, do, how they do it and 'what' they are) take priority over producing 'universal answers'.

For anybody interested in leadership of organisations... and in seeing things through a new pair of glasses.

You can read excerpts, reviews and much more information about the book at **www.meetingminds.com**.

The Leader with Seven Faces is available from Amazon, Barnes and Noble, Blackwell, WH Smith, Borders, Books Etc. and many other (online) bookshops, as well as from www.meetingminds.com.

New Leaders Wanted: Now Hiring!
12 kinds of people you must find, seduce, hire and create a job for
By Leandro Herrero

A small percentage of the workforce has the key to success. A selected group of managers make all the difference. But what are the skills these people have that enable them to create business success?

The job advertising pages don't often describe those new skills. There is a tendency to play safe and look for people with a conventional set of skills and a proven track record. However, to get spectacular success, you need an 'internal engine' of people who think and behave differently. Who are these people? Where could they be? Do I have them already or do I need to find them? You cannot ignore these questions and your number one priority should be to find these people.

New Leaders Wanted explores those new skills and new approaches to reality and will guide you in your search to find those people.

You can read excerpts, reviews and much more information about the book at **www.meetingminds.com**.

New Leaders Wanted: Now Hiring! is available from Amazon, Barnes and Noble, Blackwell, WH Smith, Borders, Books Etc. and many other (online) bookshops, as well as from www.meetingminds.com.

To order extra copies of *Disruptive Ideas* or any of our other books, contact us at sales@meetingminds.com. The books are also available from Amazon, Barnes and Noble, Blackwell, WH Smith, Borders, Books Etc. and many other (online) bookshops. For bulk orders, please contact us directly for more information on discounts and shipping costs.

Customised editions: These are special editions created for a particular audience such as a specific company or organisation. The core materials of the book are maintained, but relevant company-specific resources - such as in-house case studies or tool-kits – are added. A special foreword or tailored introduction - written either by the author or by your company's leadership - may be added as well. The book cover could also be adapted. Using modern printing technology, we can supply virtually any number of copies, from small runs to bulk production. If you are interested, please contact us.

Continue the conversation: There are many ways you can engage the author, from speaking opportunities to consulting services facilitating a change process and/or enabling your internal resources to drive change and leadership. Details can be obtained via the author's consulting website: **www.thechalfontproject.com**, through which you can also contact the author.

<meetingminds>
PO Box 1192, HP9 1YQ, United Kingdom
Tel. +44 (0)208 123 8910 - **www.meetingminds.com**
info@meetingminds.com

Lightning Source UK Ltd.
Milton Keynes UK
UKOW06f1856180815

257149UK00016B/539/P